Sparking Joyful Learning

Sparking Joyful Learning

A Teacher's Guide to Connecting Play and Reader Response

Tori K. Flint

Foreword by Karen Wohlwend

ROWMAN & LITTLEFIELD
Lanham • Boulder • New York • London

Published by Rowman & Littlefield
An imprint of The Rowman & Littlefield Publishing Group, Inc.
4501 Forbes Boulevard, Suite 200, Lanham, Maryland 20706
www.rowman.com

86-90 Paul Street, London EC2A 4NE, United Kingdom

Copyright © 2025 by Tori K. Flint

All rights reserved. No part of this book may be reproduced in any form or by any electronic or mechanical means, including information storage and retrieval systems, without written permission from the publisher, except by a reviewer who may quote passages in a review.

British Library Cataloguing in Publication Information Available

Library of Congress Cataloging-in-Publication Data Available

ISBN 9781475869811 (cloth) | ISBN 9781475869828 (paperback) | ISBN 9781475869835 (epub)

∞™ The paper used in this publication meets the minimum requirements of American National Standard for Information Sciences—Permanence of Paper for Printed Library Materials, ANSI/NISO Z39.48-1992.

Contents

Foreword *by Karen Wohlwend*   vii

Introduction   ix

1. The Importance of Children's Literature   1
2. Putting Play to Work: Implementing Responsive Play in the Classroom   15
3. Connecting Playful Reader Response to Classroom Literacy Goals   37
4. Observing, Documenting, and Assessing Literacy Learning   55
5. Play(ing) across the Day   67

References   75

About the Author   83

Foreword

This is the book we've been waiting for! In this insightful and practical guide, Tori K. Flint shows teachers what they can do to bring their reading curriculum to life through *responsive play*, that is, playful interactions with books. In clear, concise, compelling, and, most importantly, classroom-friendly terms, *Sparking Joyful Learning: A Teacher's Guide to Connecting Play and Reader Response* provides a step-by-step guide that walks teachers through curricular components of play that allow children to really get to know stories by immersing themselves in books.

We've known for decades that play is a powerful and natural way to deepen children's comprehension of books. More than 25 years ago, literacy researcher Deborah Wells Rowe (1998) showed that preschool children's comprehension of books improved when they had regular opportunities to act out books with toys. Play provides a way for young children to dramatize storylines, take a character's perspective, and explore the text's meanings by "walking around inside the story." Similarly, I've worked to demonstrate the curricular and academic value of play as a literacy to show how it provides children accessible and rich opportunities to story together. Play is a first literacy of children—an embodied way of storying, enacted by children and for children, to understand and participate in everyday worlds (Wohlwend, 2011). Building on a broad and well-established foundation of play research, Tori grounds her fresh take on playful reading in books, imagination, and joy. Yes, joy! She draws a sharp distinction between classrooms that foster joyful engagements through play with books and classrooms where reading is joyless and tedious, driven by procedures in top-down mandates.

This book couldn't be more timely, coming to us just at a time when the need to revitalize literacy learning is urgent. Despite the wealth of evidence on play's value for active and cooperative learning, time for play in schools is often equated with recess, a curricular "extra"—a frill in this no-nonsense era of education. The intense focus on high-stakes standardized testing in early grades has all but pushed play out of early childhood classrooms (Wohlwend, 2023). When play leaves the classroom, it takes with it a crucial avenue for developing children's comprehension. Tori's book catalogs easy yet powerful ways to build on children's play expertise to develop their abilities to understand characterization, storylines, dialogue, and meanings.

In this book, readers will find convincing rationales for strengthening literacy curriculum through playful reader response. They'll also find practical guidelines for implementing responsive play, clear workable plans for organizing classrooms, examples that connect play to literacy skills, and strategies for assessing the literacy learning that happens during play. Tori provides a treasure trove of playful reader-response ideas and actual classroom examples for inspiring play with children's literature and encouraging playful reader response. My hope is that someday, play will be an indispensable part of read-aloud lessons in every early childhood classroom. In *Sparking Joyful Learning*, Tori has taken a giant step toward helping our youngest children to have regular opportunities to story together and grow their comprehension skills using the literacy they know best: play.

—Karen Wohlwend

Introduction

Nathan, Carlos, and Daniel gather in the library corner of our first-grade classroom to read the big book *Ten Dogs in the Window* by Claire Masurel (2000). They kneel on the carpet with the book laid out in front of them and scoot close together so that they can all see the illustrations. Daniel is in the middle, with Nathan and Carlos on either side of him. I watch from the writing table near the library corner, trying not to be noticed.

"Ten dogs in the window . . . ," Daniel reads out loud, using his finger to track the print beneath the illustration. Carlos turns the oversized page and Daniel continues to read. As they follow along, they realize that on each page, the book presents a scenario in which the new character chooses a dog from the window to take home.

"Let's *play* the story!" says Carlos, eyes wide. "Yah!" the others cheer. They continue to read together and make predictions about which dog will be chosen next and they turn the reading engagement into a game. As a new character is presented on each page, the children race to point to the dog that they think the character will choose.

"That one!" Nathan shouts as he quickly points to a dog with a long face that strikingly resembles the woman in the illustration, "because they look the same." Daniel turns the page so they can see if Nathan's prediction is right. "You won that one!" Carlos exclaims as they all laugh and continue to read, talk, and play together.

"Huh," I whisper to myself.

***

The interesting thing about this is that these students don't really enjoy reading, not in the general, "classroom" sense. Perhaps it's because they need a lot of reading support. Maybe they don't see themselves as readers, or maybe they still haven't found enough books that they truly enjoy. Whatever the reason, most of the time, reading is not fun for them despite my best efforts. You know these students. They throw their arms down to their sides, dramatically tilt their heads back, tightly squish their eyes closed, and sigh loudly when it's time for reading groups or independent reading. So what was I witnessing here? Could I use this? The wheels start turning.

***

I walk over to the library corner and sit on the carpet in front of the group. "Hey, what are you doing?" I ask, inquisitively. Thinking they are in trouble for playing, Daniel immediately says, "Nothing, just reading." "Tell me about your game, it looks interesting!" I say, smiling to let them know they aren't in trouble. Relieved, Carlos smiles and says, "We made it playing!" "Yah, a game!" Nathan shares excitedly.

They start at the beginning of the story and share how they figured out that the dogs look like their owners. They point to each word and read each page carefully (in chorus), tell me which dog belongs with which owner, and share who guessed correctly for each page in their game. "I got the first one!" Nathan says, smiling and nodding his head proudly. "That's so cool! I like how you made the reading into a game like that!" I say. And I mean it.

***

As a teacher, you *live* for moments like this, when your students are engaged and genuinely excited about reading. You want to build on the moment, keep it going somehow. You hope to bottle that magic and sprinkle a bit around the classroom each day. But what was it that I was watching exactly? This scenario had played out in my class before—children reading and talking and playing together in the library corner—but I never took the time to really watch it, to figure out what it meant, what it *could* mean.

JUMPING INTO PLAYFUL READER RESPONSE

And so it began. I stepped out of the boundaries of my regular classroom literacy instruction and jumped feetfirst into the magical, imaginary world of playful reader response. Once I started to watch the students, I mean *really* watch them, I was struck by how much play they "snuck into" their partner reading time.

Julianna and Lucia would become the characters and create and act out alternative endings to the stories they read together. Noah and Diego would pretend to be the illustrators of the books, painting and discussing the different scenes on the pages. Gabriel would narrate the story while Zoe sang about what each character was doing, turning it into a mini-Broadway musical. It was beautiful. All of it.

So, I set out to make play a key component of reading in our classroom—because it already was. Let's be clear: the journey was not smooth. Play was not really "allowed" in the classroom, not at my school anyway, and I didn't have any solid information on the topic yet. I began to scour the internet for resources to share with parents and administrators—to let them know that children's playful responses to books could actually lead to literacy learning and growth and to show them that what I was doing was meaningful.

Finding this material proved to be a bit overwhelming, though. I would do exhaustive searches and find a wealth of information related to children's play and play–literacy connections, to reader response, or to using children's literature in the classroom—*separately*—but not a lot that *combined* these topics. I often had to alter the ideas and strategies in a way that merged them together, but I was determined to make it work.

Throughout my exploration of playful reader response, I found some valuable resources, but mainly I followed the children's lead; after all, they are the experts on play. I encouraged them to read and play when they were working on reading with a partner in class. I observed their creative transactions, and I talked with them about the ways that their play supported their reading and their learning.

The various resources I found and the ones I stitched together eventually convinced parents and administrators to get on board, and the students flourished. Our morning literacy block was joyful, vibrant, and playful—sprinkled with magic. It wasn't until years later, though, when I began my PhD program in early literacy, that I was fully able to understand the immense power of children's playful reading responses. My overarching goal in writing this book is to offer you the knowledge that I gained on my journey through the world of playful reader response. To do this, I want to share three things.

First, I want to give you relevant background information on children's play as a form of reader response by offering theories and research that support its use at school. Then I want to share practical ideas and resources for finding and using diverse children's literature and implementing playful reader response in your classroom in a way that aligns to literacy goals, standards, and assessments. Finally, I hope to encourage you to critically reflect on the ways that you can further support children's play in the classroom.

Throughout this book, I share classroom stories and anecdotes from my journey, make connections to research on children's playful reader response, and offer suggestions and resources that I found helpful (and not so helpful) along the way. Ultimately, I hope to leave you with a clear understanding of the potential of children's playful responses to literature in the classroom context.

WHAT THE RESEARCH TELLS US

After sharing a note in my weekly newsletter about how I planned to implement playful reader response in our classroom, a parent came to me one morning before school. She looked concerned and said that she wasn't sure that "just letting the kids play" would help her child learn in the long run. She went on to suggest that if her daughter was just "playing around with books," then she wasn't "really" reading, so she was confused as to how it would all work.

I was surprised by this, though I probably shouldn't have been. After all, playful reader response was new to all of us. What was clear, though, was that we seemed to be working from different definitions of "play." There was obviously a need to clarify concepts and terms before we moved forward on this journey together.

Just as I needed to take time to clarify important definitions for the parents (and also for the children and the administrators), it is important that I share with you how I define key terms and concepts so that we can begin from a place of shared understanding. Let's take a look at the different components of playful reader response and explore what the research tells us about each of them so that we are all on the same page.

Children's Play

The good thing about the term "play" is that there is not just one accepted definition. It is open to interpretation, making it flexible in its use in the classroom context. The bad thing about the term "play" is that there is not just one accepted definition. It is open to interpretation, making it confusing and easily misunderstood, especially in the classroom context, as noted in my exchange with the concerned parent.

The definition of children's play that I use in this book is drawn, firstly, from a broad understanding of play as a voluntary and pleasurable experience that often incorporates imagined and creative engagements and/or interactions with others (Nourot, 1998). In order to also highlight children's play in the *classroom* setting, I interweave this definition with one that defines this type of play as a social practice in which children create imagined circumstances and settings by "recontextualizing classroom realities and maintaining a not-real frame" (Wohlwend, 2013b, p. 80).

This combined definition highlights the joyful, creative, and social aspects of play while also noting the ways that children create imaginative, make-believe spaces and contexts at school by reframing the realities of their classroom environments.

Now that you know how I am broadly defining play, let me share with you how theories and research on young children's learning support my interpretation of play in the classroom. Sociocultural theories suggest that children are part of multiple social and cultural worlds (Flint, 2020b; Heath, 1983; Lave & Wenger, 1991). Within the sociocultural framework, play is viewed as promoting cognitive, emotional, and social development (Bodrova & Leong, 2007; Vygotsky, 1978).

Sociocultural research further suggests that play is the predominant narrative of childhood and is *essential* to children's learning (Gaskins, 2014). Play is seen as a way for children to negotiate and navigate relationships, to construct and "try on" multiple identities, and to explore various social constructs (Gee, 2012; Kuby & Vaughn, 2015; Wohlwend, 2012).

When children play in the *classroom*, they are able to connect to and explore various aspects of their worlds, expanding their opportunities for learning (Wohlwend, 2013a). As such, children actively contribute to classroom learning landscapes through their cooperative interactions, including their talk and their play (Bakhtin, 1986). Ultimately, children's play allows them the freedom to demonstrate and share their knowledge, experiences, emotions, and feelings and to individually and/or cooperatively create and cultivate new and important spaces for learning, growth, and, importantly, joy (Flint & Adams, 2024; Leander & Rowe, 2006).

Extending the sociocultural perspective on play and children's learning and development in the classroom is the concept of *funds of knowledge* (Gonzalez et al., 2005). Children's and families' funds of knowledge include the "essential cultural practices and bodies of knowledge and information that houses use to survive, to get ahead, or to thrive" (Moll, 1992, p. 21), including their language(s), family literacies, culture, religion, work contexts, cooking practices, and so on. This knowledge is carried to school by children and transferred to the classroom in various ways.

Because children's funds of knowledge are often deeply embedded within their playful interactions, teachers can leverage play as a means to weave students' home lives and experiences into the curriculum in ways that can help them develop language, literacy, and school-related skills in meaningful contexts (Riojas-Cortez, 2001).

Play–Literacy Connections

As children draw on their experiences, their family lives, and their home cultures to explore and interpret their worlds in the classroom, they also make important connections between play and literacy. In contemporary times, literacy goes beyond standard reading and writing practices. Children's literacies are made up of *multiple* modes (Kress, 2003; New London Group, 1996), including (but not limited to) textual, visual, auditory/sonic, sensual, artistic, linguistic, gestural, embodied, affective, and digital modalities (Boldt & Leander, 2020; Dernikos, 2020; Kumpulainen et al., 2020; Leander & Boldt, 2013; Marsh, 2017; Thiel, 2015).

Accordingly, in the classroom, children often draw from their funds of knowledge, along with previous literacy and/or play engagements, books, technology/digital engagements, media, popular culture, toys/games, and so on, to create meaningful literacy connections that inform and strengthen their understanding(s). Within these connections, play can be seen as a vehicle for children's literacy learning and meaning making.

Studies on play–literacy connections demonstrate the various ways that children engage in literacy practices as they use play to make sense of literacy-rich environments like the classroom (Flint & Adams, 2024; Wohlwend, 2013a, 2013b). For example, research has shown that young children make sense of reading and writing as they integrate literacy into classroom centers and play events by taking orders in make-believe restaurants, creating store receipts, making signs, and so on (Owocki, 1999).

Numerous classroom studies support these findings, demonstrating positive links between play and literacy in the areas of literacy acquisition, reading skills, comprehension, emergent writing, vocabulary and linguistic skills, and narrative competence (Christie & Roskos, 2009; Saracho & Spodek, 2006). This research further highlights children's play as an essential component of children's literacy learning and development (Paley, 2004).

Reader Response

Similar to the ways that children draw from their knowledge and experiences to inform their play and to build play–literacy connections, readers use their past experiences with literacy, language, and life as the "raw materials out of which to shape the new experience symbolized on the page" (Rosenblatt, 1938, p. 25). The transactional theory suggests that reading is a two-way, *transactional* process between a reader and a text wherein the text informs the reader and the reader draws from their knowledge and their past experiences in order to infuse the text with meaning and to construct understanding (Rosenblatt, 1938, 1978).

As children read books in the classroom, they are engaged in various meaning-making processes, and through their reading responses, they are able to demonstrate their understanding(s) (Flint & Adams, 2018; Pantaleo, 2008; Sipe, 2008). Teachers often use reader response in their classrooms in the form of discussion, writing, and/or drawing so that children can share these multifaceted processes and understandings. Beyond these standard forms of reader response, research also suggests that dramatic story retellings/reenactments can greatly support young children's literacy learning (Adomat, 2009).

Through dramatic response, children can act out and retell stories in their own words, giving insight into their analyses of characters and storylines. This form of reader response is highly engaging and allows children to negotiate diverse perspectives as they interpret, play/replay, and retell stories in various ways.

Research further suggests that young children's book-related dramatic play of this sort is a "context for literacy learning . . . and a process of comprehending books, expressing one's reactions, experiencing books in affective and kinesthetic ways, as well as a means of inquiry and participating in literacy events" (Rowe, 1998, p. 11). This type of playful, book-related dramatic response enriches children's learning by expanding the possibilities for how they create and express meaning and understanding in relation to children's literature.

BRINGING IT ALL TOGETHER

So far, I have shared with you my definition of play along with what the research tells us about children's play, play–literacy connections, and reader response in the classroom. Now let's tie all these pieces together. Drawing from the transactional theory and extending the research on play, play–literacy connections, and dramatic reader response, I have constructed a new framework that connects these concepts and highlights children's play as a meaningful and joyful form of reader response, which I call *responsive play*.

Young children often use play in ways similar to the ways that adult readers use language and writing to make connections to, reflect on, and respond to books (Rowe, 1998). Through their voluntary, playful responses to literature in the classroom—their responsive play—children can both participate in and create their own imaginary situations and draw from their personal experiences to explore their worlds, the story world, and the world around them (Rosenblatt, 1938). This allows them to effectively merge their reading transactions with their own experiences in order to transform these into meaningful responses and understandings.

Because children's language and literacy skills are developed through the interconnected links between books and their playful transactions with and responses to stories, this type of play provides various opportunities for literacy learning and meaning making in the classroom context (Flint 2020a, 2020b; Flint & Adams, 2018; Rowe, 1998, 2007).

IGNITING THE SPARK

Now that we are on the same page, let me share a few thoughts before you read further. This book is an attempt to outline what worked for me on my long journey through the world of playful reader response. As you move forward through this text, I hope you find that you are able to use the information I share as a resource as you embark on your own journey through responsive play.

Before you begin, have you seen the movie *Castaway*? In this film, Tom Hanks's character, who is stranded on a deserted island, is finally able to create the one thing that he needs to ensure his survival: fire. Once he lights the fire, he dances like a child on the beach, excited, relieved, and motivated to survive—to live. All it took was one spark.

As you continue reading, keep in mind that for children, responding to books through play can be the spark that ignites imaginative literacy learning in your classroom. And keep in mind that *you* have the power to harness that spark, to tend to it, to nurture it, and to fan it into a raging fire of joyful meaning making. Let the students dance on the beaches of your classroom, to learn—to thrive. Let them play.

1

The Importance of Children's Literature

As books are essential components of literacy instruction and playful reader response, this chapter highlights the importance of children's literature, including the value of reading for fun and joy. Because each child deserves to see themselves and others within the books in their classroom library, this chapter also discusses the need to use high-quality, diverse children's literature in the classroom; suggests various resources for finding and using these books; and provides relevant examples to guide you as you ignite the spark of imaginative and joyful literacy learning in your classroom.

READ, PLAY, LAUGH

Gholdy Muhammad (2023) suggests that cultivating joy is the ultimate goal of teaching and learning. Her work reminds us that living and learning, in the classroom environment, is about more than just test scores, though outside and administrative pressures may suggest otherwise. So what is joy? And how does it "fit" in the classroom?

Joy, in this sense, is coming together as a classroom community. It's tapping into each child's humanity and genius, honoring student's histories, and rejoicing in their potential. It's creating classroom spaces that support humanizing and imaginative experiences. In your literacy instruction, joy can also look like reading and responding to diverse books in authentic and playful ways.

Cultivating Imagination and Joy

Children's literature, in school contexts, is often viewed simply as instructional material used to teach reading comprehension and writing skills. Since children's books are so frequently used for teaching purposes (with great success), it can be easy to forget that literature has value in and of itself, beyond enhancing children's language and literacy learning. Books are fun, too! They offer enjoyment, humor, laughter, and opportunities for personal connections. When paired with playful reading responses, they can offer limitless opportunities for imagination and joy.

When reading and responding to books, children often go through a process of playful and imaginative trial and error in which they try on and try out different thought processes, behaviors, identities, and actions in order to "work out" their probable effects—but also for the sake of fun. Storybooks promote this type of playful experimentation because they offer such a variety of unique experiences for children to *live through* as they enter story worlds, *become* various characters, and engage with(in) and through the books (Rosenblatt, 1938, 1978).

Through literature, children can create and participate in imaginary situations and draw from their literacies, histories, and personal experiences to explore their world, the story world, and the world around them. This frees them to playfully respond to books in various ways, allowing fun and joy to guide the reading-and-responding process.

So how can you cultivate this type of joy in your literacy instruction? First, you must consider the classroom reading and response contexts that promote and hinder fun and imagination.

What Promotes Imaginative and Joyful Reading and Response?

- Choices (in books/book formats, partners, reading spaces)
- Access (to a variety of diverse books)
- Time (ample time for reading and responding to stories)
- Space (ample and comfortable spaces for reading and response)
- Opportunities for social interaction (literature circles, reader's theater, reading to pets, reading with partners/groups, book clubs)
- Family (encouragement to read and respond to stories with family members)
- Opportunities to respond to books in various ways (discussion, art/photography, writing, video production, drama, movement, play)

What Makes Reading and Responding Joyless?

- Lack of choice (in books/book formats, partners, reading spaces)
- Lack of access (to diverse books)

- Lack of time (for reading and responding to stories)
- Lack of space(s) to read and respond to stories
- Lack of opportunities to read with/to others
- Book logs (these can sometimes position reading as an unappealing required chore/task/assignment)
- Tests/quizzes on readings (this can often lead to lack of reading and response motivation)
- Mandatory book reports (while some children may enjoy writing book reports, these may also hinder creative reading responses and position reading and responding as an unappealing required chore or task)

Reading and responding to books through play, simply for the joy of it, will help support the children in your classroom to use their imaginations, think critically and creatively, and feel authentically engaged in the reading process. In order for children to better understand themselves and others while reading and responding through imaginative and joyful play in your classroom, it is also important that they see themselves on the bookshelf of your classroom library.

THE NEED FOR QUALITY DIVERSE CHILDREN'S LITERATURE

Classroom communities are made up of children and teachers from various backgrounds and with diverse experiences. As such, all children should be able to find their lives and experiences reflected in the books they read at school. To help children make valuable connections to and with storybooks, characters, and authors and illustrators, books that are reflective of the various identities of the children in your classroom community (and beyond) should be readily available.

These should include (but not be limited to) books that highlight various diverse and positive depictions of:

- Race
- Culture
- Gender
- Language(s)
- The LGBTQIA+ community
- People with disabilities
- Families
- Friendships
- Religion(s)
- Socioeconomic status
- Lived experiences

In her well-known article "Mirrors, Windows, and Sliding Glass Doors," Dr. Rudine Sims Bishop (1990) notes,

> Books are sometimes windows, offering views of worlds that may be real or imagined, familiar or strange. These windows are also sliding glass doors, and readers have only to walk through in imagination to become part of whatever world has been created or recreated by the author. When lighting conditions are just right, however, a window can also be a mirror. Literature transforms human experience and reflects it back to us, and in that reflection we can see our own lives and experiences as part of the larger human experience. Reading, then, becomes a means of self-affirmation, and readers often seek their mirrors in books. (p. ix)

This suggests that books can transform the human experience and reflect it back to readers as mirrors, offer views of familiar/unfamiliar and real/imagined worlds as windows, and allow readers to walk into and become a part of the worlds created by the writers and illustrators as sliding glass doors.

This groundbreaking work further asks us to consider *who* has multiple mirrors and *whose* mirrors are singular, distorted, broken, or missing. It also begs us to consider which readers must "walk through texts in search of empowering images they may never find" and to reflect on the messages we foreground when those images are absent or stereotypical (Toliver, 2021, p. 29). Just as there are multiple aspects to our identities, there are various ways that we can see ourselves reflected or *not* reflected in books.

What Can Teachers Do?

When certain voices and stories are missing from the books used in the classroom, children who are left out may feel undervalued or invisible. Further, children whose lives are constantly and continuously reflected might gain a false sense of their own importance, a "sense that they are the privileged 'norm'" (Bishop, 2016, p. 120). To counteract this, teachers can purposefully collect and use diverse, relevant, inclusive, and high-quality children's literature that gives students opportunities to see themselves and others in various contexts (Keefer & Flint, 2023).

By using diverse books in this way, you can include and *highlight* the experiences and histories of children, allow *all* students to see themselves and others within the pages of the books shared in the classroom space, share worlds and possibilities beyond the pages, and support students as they interact with, in, and through new contexts and realities (Jiménez, 2021).

To do this, you must first actively consider and take account of what representation is already present in your classroom library and, perhaps more importantly, consider what is missing. You must then ask yourself how you can expand these options to include a wider range of human experiences.

Here are some questions to consider when determining how inclusive your current classroom library is:

- Does my classroom library reflect the reading preferences of my students?
- Whose voices and experiences are represented/centered in the books on my shelves?
  - Whose voices and experiences are marginalized or missing?
- Which author/illustrator voices are represented or centered?
  - Which author/illustrator voices are marginalized or missing?
- Which languages are represented in the books on my shelves?
  - Which languages are marginalized or missing?

As you surely know, teachers are under tremendous pressure to cover expansive mandated literacy and English language arts content and curricula. There is a strong focus on standards, test preparation, test scores, benchmarks, and data, and these things, undoubtedly, shape your daily literacy instruction. As a teacher, you work hard to manage all these things *and* to keep your students engaged and interested in reading. It's hard work! How can you be asked to do *more*?

While the task of (re)building a diverse classroom library may seem daunting, it is important to know that including diverse books can improve your students' learning in various ways. When your classroom library is diverse and inclusive, you are inviting and supporting students to do the following:

- Bring their "full selves" to the classroom
- Connect to stories, characters, authors, and illustrators
- Construct meaning through stories
- Build understandings of themselves and others
- Explore and analyze their own worlds and the world around them
- Engage with texts in personal and meaningful ways
- Enjoy reading
- Discuss important issues and topics
- Engage with and respond to stories in various ways (writing, art, play)
- Draw from lived experiences to respond to stories
- Utilize their imaginations

Children often view books as maps. They "create, through the stories they are given, an atlas of their world, of their relationship with others, of their possible destinations" (Myers, 2014, n.p.). Providing diverse and inclusive children's literature in the classroom, as maps, can offer children alternative landscapes in which to see themselves and others, leading them, as readers, to new and undiscovered locations (Marshall, 2016). By including diverse books in your classroom library, you can help your students chart exciting routes to new destinations and support them on their playful reading journeys.

Note

Keep in mind that in today's political landscape, which increasingly includes bans on books that discuss issues of race and racism; include LGBTQ+ authors/illustrators, characters, and themes; foreground Characters of Color; include languages other than English; or highlight religions other than Christianity, it may be difficult to introduce and use inclusive and diverse children's literature in your classroom.

While including these types of books in your classroom library is certainly important, it is also important that you know the laws and policies of your school, district, and state as you navigate their use and inclusion in your literacy instruction. Unfortunately, these laws and mandates have real consequences for educators and can limit which books you can have/use in your classroom.

Also consider that some laws and mandates may actually *help* support you as you (re)build your diverse classroom library. Anti-bullying/harassment and nondiscrimination laws and policies may support your use of inclusive children's literature in the classroom.

RESOURCES

Critically choosing and purposefully using diverse and inclusive children's literature can simultaneously provide students access to mirrors, windows, and sliding glass doors and connect them to joyful literacy learning. But *finding* high-quality diverse books can sometimes be difficult.

Below is a list of various resources, websites, books, and awards to help you locate high-quality, diverse, and inclusive literature to use in your classroom (in alphabetical order):

- American Indians in Children's Literature (https://americanindiansinchildrensliterature.blogspot.com)
- American Library Association—disability-focused authors/texts (https://www.ala.org/awardsgrants/awards/1/all_years)

- American Library Association's Rainbow Book List—LGBTQIA+-focused authors/texts: (https://glbtrt.ala.org/rainbowbooks)
- Bank Street Center for Children's Literature (https://www.bankstreet.edu/library/center-for-childrens-literature)
- Children's Book Awards (https://libguides.bc.edu/c.php?g=43969&p=279270), (https://www.socialstudies.org/awards/septima-clark-book-awards)
- Children's Literature Assembly (CLA) of the National Council of Teachers of English (NCTE) (https://www.childrensliteratureassembly.org)
- Children's Literature Association (https://www.childlitassn.org/resources)
- Diverse Book Finder—multicultural and bi-/multilingual books (https://diversebookfinder.org)
- Humanizing Stories: @healingfictions (X/Twitter)
- Kibooka: Kid's Books by Korean Americans (https://kibooka.com)
- Latinxs in Kid Lit (https://latinosinkidlit.com)
- Lee & Low Books (https://www.leeandlow.com)
- National Council for the Social Studies (NCSS): Notable Trade Books for Young People (https://www.socialstudies.org/notable-trade-books/2023)
- Raising Luminaries (https://bookshop.org/categories/m/children-s-books)
- Reading the Rainbow: LGBTQ-Inclusive Literacy Instruction in the Elementary Classroom (Ryan & Hermann-Wilmarth, 2018) (https://www.tcpress.com/reading-the-rainbow-9780807759332)
- Social Justice Books: A Teaching for Change Project (https://socialjusticebooks.org/booklists)
- We Are Kid Lit Collective (https://wtpsite.wordpress.com)
- We Need Diverse Books (https://diversebooks.org/resources-old/where-to-find-diverse-books)

Note that this list is not exhaustive. There are many wonderful books, websites, and blogs that can help you find authentic, well-written, diverse, and inclusive children's literature to use in your classroom.

EXAMPLES

Below are some examples of high-quality, inclusive, and diverse children's literature that may pair well with imaginative and playful reader response in the classroom (see Tables 1.1 to 1.9). Many of these books are drawn from the resources noted above.

Table 1.1 Books with LGBTQIA+ Characters, Themes, and/or Authors/Illustrators

And Tango Makes Three by Justin Richardson and Peter Parnell, illustrated by Henry Cole (2005)

Bathe the Cat by Alice B. McGinty, illustrated by David Roberts (2022)

Calvin by J. R. Ford and Vanessa Ford, illustrated by Kalya Harren (2021)

Forever Home: A Dog and Boy Love Story by Henry Cole (2022)

Grandad's Camper by Harry Woodgate (2021)

My Footprints by Bao Phi and Basia Tran, illustrated by Ngoc Diep Barbara Tran (2019)

My Rainbow by Trinity Neal and Deshanna Neal, illustrated by Art Twink (2020)

Our Subway Baby by Peter Mercurio, illustrated by Leo Espinosa (2020)

Sewing the Rainbow by Gayle E. Pitman, illustrated by Clifton Brown (2018)

Note: See "Children's Literature References" in the References section for full citations.

Table 1.2 Books That Highlight the Disability Experience

A Friend for Henry by Jenn Bailey, illustrated by Mika Song (2019)

A Sky-Blue Bench by Bahram Rahman, illustrated by Peggy Collins (2021)

A Splash of Red: The Life and Art of Horace Pippen by Jen Bryant, illustrated by Melissa Sweet (2013)

A Walk in the Words by Hudson Talbott (2021)

Hooway for Wodney Wat by Helen Lester, illustrated by Lunn Munsinger (2002)

I Talk Like a River by Jordan Scott, illustrated by Sydney Smith (2020)

In the Blue by Erin Hourigan (2022)

My City Speaks by Darren Lebeuf, illustrated by Ashely Barron (2021)

The Pirate of Kindergarten by George Ella Lyon, illustrated by Lynne Avril (2010)

The Remember Balloons by Jesse Oliveros, illustrated by Dana Wulfekotte (2018)

Note: See "Children's Literature References" in the References section for full citations.

Table 1.3 Translingual and Bilingual Books

Abuela by Arthur Dorros, illustrated by Elisa Klevin (1997)
Areli is a Dreamer by Areli Morales, illustrated by Luisa Uribe (2021)
Birds on Wishbone Street by Suzanne Del Rizzo (2021)
Daniel and Ismail by Juan Pablo Iglesias, illustrated by Alex Peris (2019)
Drawn Together by Minh Lê, illustrated by Dan Santat (2018)
Dreamers by Yuyi Morales (2018)
I Dream of Popo by Livia Blackburne, illustrated by Julia Kuo (2021)
Marisol McDonald Doesn't Match/Marisol McDonald No Combina (English and Spanish ed.) by Monica Brown, illustrated by Sara Palacios (2011)
My Papi Has a Motorcycle by Isabel Quintero, illustrated by Zeke Peña (2019)
Stepping Stones: A Refugee Family's Journey by Marie Margariet Ruurs, translated by Falah Raheem, illustrated by Nizr Ali Vadr (2016)

Note: See "Children's Literature References" in the References section for full citations.

Table 1.4 Books with Black Characters and/or Created by Black Authors/Illustrators

Amazing Grace by Mary Hoffman, illustrated by Caroline Binch (1991)
Crown: An Ode to the Fresh Cut by Derrick Barnes, illustrated by Gordon C. James (2017)
Hair Love by Matthew A. Cherry, illustrated by Vashti Harrison (2019)
I Am Enough by Grace Byers, illustrated by Keurah A. Bobo (2018)
I Am Every Good Thing by Derrick Barnes, illustrated by Gordon C. James (2020)
Sulwe by Lupita Nyong'o, illustrated by Vashti Harrison (2019)
Tar Beach by Faith Ringgold (1996)
The Snowy Day by Ezra Jack Keats (1962)
The Year We Learned to Fly by Jacqueline Woodson, illustrated by Rafael López (2022)
Visiting Day by Jacqueline Woodson, illustrated by James E. Ransome (2015)

Note: See "Children's Literature References" in the References section for full citations.

Table 1.5 Books with Indigenous/Native Characters and/or by Indigenous/Native Authors/Illustrators

Birdsong by Julie Flett (2019)
Dancing with Our Ancestors (Sk'ad'a Stories Series, Vol. 4) by Sara Florence Davidson and Robert Davidson, illustrated by Janine Gibbons (2022)
Fry Bread by Kevin Noble Maillard, illustrated by Juana Martinez-Neal (2019)
My Powerful Hair by Carole Lindstrom, illustrated by Steph Littlebird (2023)
On the Trapline by David Robertson, illustrated by Julie Fett (2021)
The Range Eternal by Louise Erdrich, illustrated by Steve Johnson and Lou Fancher (2020)
The Secret Pocket by Peggy Janicki, illustrated by Carrielynn Victor (2023)
Too Much: My Great Big Native Family by Laurel Goodluck, illustrated by Bridget George (2024)
We Are Water Protectors by Carole Lindstrom, illustrated by Michaela Goade (2020)
When We Gather (Ostadahlisiha): A Cherokee Tribal Feast by Andrea L. Rogers, illustrated by Madelyn Goodnight (2024)

Note: See "Children's Literature References" in the References section for full citations.

Table 1.6 Books with Latine(o/a/x) Characters and/or Created by Latine(o/a/x) Authors/Illustrators

A Movie in My Pillow: Una Pelicula en mi Almohada by Jorge Argueta, illustrated by Elizabeth Gomez (2007)
Chato's Kitchen by Gary Soto, illustrated by Susan Guevara (1997)
Island Born by Junot Díaz, illustrated by Leo Espinosa (2018)
Last Stop on Market Street by Matt de la Peña, illustrated by Christian Robinson (2015)
Lucia the Luchadora by Cynthia Leonor Garza, illustrated by Alyssa Bermudez (2017)
Martina the Beautiful Cockroach: A Cuban Folktale by Carmen Agra Deedy, illustrated by Michael Austin (2014)
Niño Wrestles the World by Yuyi Morales (2015)
Paletero Man by Lucky Diaz, illustrated by Micah Player (2021)
Pancakes for Breakfast by Tomie dePaola (2018)
Too Many Tamales by Gary Soto, illustrated by Ed Martinez (1996)

Note: See "Children's Literature References" in the References section for full citations.

Table 1.7 Books with Asian/Asian-American, Native Hawaiian/Pacific Islander Characters and/or by Asian/Asian-American, Native Hawaiian/Pacific Islander Authors/Illustrators

Dim Sum for Everyone by Grace Lin (2014)
Eyes That Kiss in the Corners by Joanna Ho, illustrated by Dung Ho (2021)
Grandfather's Journey by Allen Say (2008)
Ho'onani: Hula Warrior by Heather Gale, illustrated by Mika Song (2019)
My Name Is Yoon by Helen Recorvits, illustrated by Gabi Swiatkowska (2014)
The Blur by Minh Lê, illustrated by Dan Santat (2022)
The Name Jar by Yangsook Choi (2003)
The Truth about Dragons by Julie Leung, illustrated by Hanna Cha (2023)
Tiger in My Soup by Kashmira Sheth, illustrated by Jeffrey Ebbeler (2013)
Wabi Sabi by Mark Reibstein, illustrated by Ed Young (2008)

Note: See "Children's Literature References" in the References section for full citations.

Table 1.8 Books That Highlight Jewish and Muslim Experiences

Abdul's Story by Jamilah Thompkins-Bigelow, illustrated by Tiffany Rose (2022)
Beautiful Yetta the Yiddish Chicken by Daniel Pinkwater, illustrated by Jill Pinkwater (2010)
Jalepeño Bagels by Natasha Wing, illustrated by Robert Casilla (1996)
Loujain Dreams of Sunflowers by Uma Mishra-Newbery and Lina Al-Hathloul, illustrated by Rebecca Green (2022)
Mrs. Katz and Tush by Patricia Polacco (1994)
Queen of the Hanukkah Dosas by Pamela Ehrenberg, illustrated by Anjan Sarkar (2017)
Sitti's Secrets by Naomi Shihab Nye, illustrated by Nancy Carpenter (1997)
The Butterfly by Patrica Polacco (2009)
The Proudest Blue: A Story of Hijab and Family by Ibtihaj Muhammad, illustrated by S. K. Ali Hatem Aly (2019)
Yo Soy Muslim: A Father's Letter to His Daughter by Mark Gonzales, illustrated by Mehrdokht Amini (2017)

Note: See "Children's Literature References" in the References section for full citations.

Table 1.9 Award-Winning Books

From the Tops of the Trees by Kao Kalia Yan, illustrated by Rachel Wada (2021), Asian/Pacific American Award for Literature

Hot Dog by Doug Salati (2022), Caldecott Medal, American Picturebook

Knock, Knock: My Dad's Dream for Me by Daniel Beaty, illustrated by Bryan Collier (2013), Coretta Scott King Award (African American experience)

Listen: How Evelyn Glennie, a Deaf Girl, Changed Percussion by Shannon Stocker, illustrated by Devon Holzwarth (2022), Schneider Family Book Award (disability experience)

Love, Violet by Charlotte Sullivan Wild, illustrated by Charlene Chua (2022), Stonewall Book Award (LGBTQIA+ experience)

The Coquíes Still Sing: A Story of Home, Hope, and Rebuilding by Karina Nicole González, illustrated by Krystal Quiles (2022), Pura Belpré Honor Award (Latine/o/a/x experience)

The Stuff of Stars by Marion Dane Bauer, illustrated by Ekua Holmes (2018), Coretta Scott King Illustrator Award (African American experience)

The Tower of Life: How Yaffa Eliach Rebuilt Her Town by Chana Stiefel, illustrated by Susan Gal (2022), Sydney Taylor Book Award (Jewish experience)

Watercress by Andrea Wang, illustrated by Jason Chin (2021), Asian/Pacific American Award

Where Wonder Grows by Xelenaul González, illustrated by Adriana M. Garcia (2022), Pura Belpré Illustration Award (Latine/o/a/x experience)

Note: See "Children's Literature References" in the References section for full citations.

Special Notes:

- In order to avoid *problematic* texts that might exclude or stereotype people or contexts, you should prioritize books that are created by authors and illustrators who share the characteristics of the characters portrayed in their stories. By purposefully including and highlighting books created by authors and illustrators who are People of Color, have disabilities, represent the LGBTQ+ community, or are members of certain religious or cultural groups, you will be helping to ensure that the portrayals are authentic and meaningful.
- Avoid adding spine or cover labels to books or bins in your classroom library that say "multicultural," "diverse," or "POC (People of Color)." Labeling books in this way does *not* celebrate diversity; instead, it centers whiteness as the norm and declares the labeled books and the authors and the characters within those books as "different" or "other."

FINAL THOUGHTS

Because books are key components of responsive play in the classroom, this chapter has discussed children's literature in various contexts:

- Cultivating imagination and joy
- Having and using quality, diverse books

This chapter has also suggested several resources for locating quality children's literature and provided relevant examples to help you begin to (re)build your classroom library as you prepare for your responsive play journey.

As you fill your shelves with authentic, diverse, and engaging books, children will be drawn into the magical world of joyful, meaningful reading practices and playful reader response. Ultimately, your reinvigorated library will help you invite children to imaginatively respond to books as you "put play to work" in your classroom, as highlighted in the next chapter.

2

Putting Play to Work
Implementing Responsive Play in the Classroom

In the vignette in the introduction of this book, Nathan, Carlos, and Daniel responded to a book by inventing and playing a game as they read together, creating a playful social context that encouraged their understandings and their interpretations of the story and supported their meaning making. Their play motivated their collective interest in reading and understanding the story and in discussing the characters and story events, and vice versa, their understandings and interpretations of the book and their discussions of story events and illustrations informed and motivated their playful responses.

This reciprocal relationship between the children's understanding(s) of the story and their play created a unique classroom reading experience that was simultaneously fun *and* supportive of their literacy development. This joyful engagement allowed for the creation of a space within the classroom wherein the children were able to playfully practice and extend their literacy strategies and skills (like making predictions about the story). The children's creative responses reveal how play can easily mesh with emergent and early literacy practices and highlight the importance of imaginative play in the classroom.

Children are *always already* playing and learning (Dreyfus & Wrathall, 2007). The children in the introductory vignette did not need to be directed to play. They did so instinctively because play is an essential component of their culture—the culture of childhood. In the classroom, children's play is fun, but it is also their *work*. Children learn through play (Paley, 2004). This chapter will help you "play to work" in your classroom as you weave responsive play into your daily literacy instruction.

Building on the Introduction of this book and key ideas about the importance of diverse children's literature from Chapter 1, this chapter provides a practical guide for implementing the various aspects of responsive play in the classroom setting. The following sections focus on using materials to invite children into the world of playful reader response, creating space(s) and making time for play, choosing and using books and reading materials, and the "rules." This chapter concludes with suggestions for adjusting these components to meet the unique needs of each classroom.

THE SPACE-TIME-MATERIALITY CONTINUUM

Albert Einstein determined that space and time, rather than being separate and unrelated, are actually woven together into a single continuum that spans multiple dimensions. This creates a sort of space-time fabric, like a sheet or blanket. Doc Brown, from the movie *Back to the Future*, highlights the complex nature of this fabric (including the materials and people within it) when he tells Marty McFly that altering the continuum could create a time paradox, the results of which could be disastrous.

While engaging in playful reader response is certainly not as dangerous as riding in a time-traveling DeLorean, space, time, and materials are all essential pieces of the responsive play fabric.

Playing with(in) and through Materials: Invitations to Play

By allowing children to play with(in) and through books in your classroom, you can cocreate literacy spaces wherein children can relate to, connect with, and transact with stories in academically focused ways that also highlight social connection and fun. Alongside books, certain materials can act as invitations for children to share their knowledge and experiences through playful reader response and infuse these literacy spaces with learning and joy. Let's take a look at some materials that can effectively invite children into the world of responsive play.

Cutouts

Research conducted by Patricia Edmiston (Enciso) (1990, 1996) suggests that when young readers use paper cutouts (images printed from storybooks) that represent story characters, the setting, the author and illustrator, and themselves as the readers, they are better able to demonstrate their engagement with the story. Modifying this concept, various cutouts can be created and used not only to demonstrate engagement but also to invite children to respond to stories through play.

Character cutouts can invite children to "become" storybook characters and to engage in playful responses to stories *as* those characters. These images can be printed from clip art or story images found online, or they can be photographed and/or copied directly from the books in your classroom. For example, cutouts can include small, scanned images of story characters like the dragon, the prince, and the princess from the book *The Paper Bag Princess* by Robert Munsch (1980).

Reader, author, and illustrator cutouts can also be created to represent the book creators and the children themselves. Images for these cutouts can vary but should be easily identifiable to your students. For example, an image of a pencil can represent the author so that children understand that the author writes the words in the stories. An image of a paintbrush can be used to represent the illustrator, highlighting that the illustrator creates the images in the books. An image of a mirror can be used to represent the students as readers so that when they use this cutout, they can "see themselves" in the mirror *within* the stories. Images of settings can also be created.

These are simply suggestions. You will determine which images work best for your students. For example, the depiction of a pencil to represent the author of a story could easily be replaced with an image of a computer keyboard or a pen. Similarly, the image of the paintbrush used to represent the illustrator could be replaced with images of markers and crayons or with famous artists who are familiar to your students.

The cutout images can be black and white or you can choose to print them in color. You might also consider printing them in black and white and then having the children color them. You could also draw/create your own cutout images. Another great option is to have the *children* draw and create their own character, author, illustrator, reader, and setting cutouts for each book in your responsive play space(s).

Printed and created images can also be trimmed and taped to popsicle sticks for ease of use. This is a simple and inexpensive way to enhance the cutouts, and it makes them more fun for students to use. If you choose not to use popsicle sticks, you might consider gluing images on index cards, printing them on thick paper or cardstock, or finding another way to create them altogether. You may also want to laminate paper cutouts so that they last longer. Cutouts can be stored in a pencil box, tub, basket, or in sandwich bags.

Keep in mind that if you choose to use cutouts to invite children to play with(in) stories, there should be a variety of cutouts for them to choose from; and there should also be several copies of each cutout in case more than one child wants to "become" a particular character as they respond to the story through play together. Also keep in mind that the cutouts should be explained to children, but children should not be required to use them or directed on *how* to use/play with them if they choose to do so, as this might interfere with children's *authentic* play responses.

If you have the time, the means, and the ability to create more detailed or intricate cutouts or playful invitations in a completely different format, feel free to expand on the ideas and suggestions shared here. For example, if you are artistically inclined and want to include cutouts or other materials depicting elaborately painted story scenery, including happy little trees, channel your inner Bob Ross and do it!

Other Materials

Beyond the cutouts mentioned above, other items and materials can be used to effectively invite children to play in response to stories in your classroom. These include but are not limited to:

- Puppets
- Stuffed animals
- Toys
- Props (everyday objects that represent story items, like a spoon)
- Dress-up items
  - Clothes
  - Hats
  - Shoes
  - Scarfs/accessories
- Writing and art materials
- Art/drawings/photographs

Like the cutouts, these items and materials are simply playful invitations. Be sure that you explain what each item *is* but try not to direct children *how to use* the materials as they read and respond to books.

Creating Space(s) and Making Time for Playful Reader Response

Now that you have some ideas about creating and using materials to invite children into the world of responsive play, let's discuss the different literacy instruction formats that are conducive to introducing play as a form of reader response into your classroom.

Workshop/Centers Formats

In the standard workshop/centers format (see Table 2.1), the teacher presents a whole-group focus lesson after which students, in small groups, rotate through various centers or stations to read and to practice their literacy skills and strategies in various ways. During these rotations, the

Table 2.1 Standard Workshop/Centers Format

Standard Workshop/Center Component	Time Frame	Description
Focus lesson	5 to 10 minutes	Whole group. The teacher briefly instructs children on a specific literacy skill/strategy. Children then go to their first center/station.
Rotation 1	Approximately 15 minutes	Children work in the center/station, and when the bell rings/timer goes off, they clean up and move to the next center in the rotation.
Rotation 2	Approximately 15 minutes	Children work in the center/station, and when the bell rings/timer goes off, they clean up and move to the next center in the rotation.
Rotation 3	Approximately 15 minutes	Children work in the center/station, and when the bell rings/timer goes off, they clean up and move to the next center in the rotation.
Rotation 4	Approximately 15 minutes	Children work in the center/station, and when the bell rings/timer goes off, they clean up and move to the next center in the rotation.
Rotation 5	Approximately 15 minutes	Children work in the center/station, and when the bell rings/timer goes off, they clean up and move to the next center in the rotation.
Reflect/share/closing meeting	3 to 5 minutes	Teacher/students gather and reflect on and share what they worked on in the centers. The teacher reemphasizes the literacy skill/strategy taught in the opening focus lesson.

teacher can meet with individuals or small groups of children to assess learning and to instruct. After rotations are complete, the class comes back together for a final whole-group share/reflection. This format can vary in many ways, fewer centers can be utilized, and less or more time in each center can be allotted as needed.

In the alternative workshop/centers format (see Table 2.2), a minilesson is done at the beginning and then again after *each* center rotation,

Table 2.2 Alternative Workshop/Centers Format

Alternative Workshop/ Center Component	Time Frame	Description
Mini-lesson	2 to 3 minutes	Whole group. The teacher very briefly instructs children on a specific literacy skill/strategy. Children then move to their first center/station.
Rotation 1	Approximately 15 minutes	Children work in the center/station, and when the bell rings/timer goes off, they clean up and return to the meeting area for another mini-lesson (continued from the previous mini-lesson or on a new topic).
Mini-lesson	2 to 3 minutes	Whole group. The teacher very briefly instructs children on a specific literacy skill/strategy. Children then move to their next center/station.
Rotation 2	Approximately 15 minutes	Children work in the center/station, and when the bell rings/timer goes off, they clean up and return to the meeting area for another mini-lesson (continued from the previous mini-lesson or on a new topic).
Mini-lesson	2 to 3 minutes	Whole group. The teacher very briefly instructs children on a specific literacy skill/strategy. Children then move to their next center/station.
Rotation 3	Approximately 15 minutes	Children work in the center/station, and when the bell rings/timer goes off, they clean up and return to the meeting area for another mini-lesson (continued from the previous mini-lesson or on a new topic).
Mini-lesson	2 to 3 minutes	Whole group. The teacher very briefly instructs children on a specific literacy skill/strategy. Children then move to their next center/station.

(Continued)

Table 2.2 (Continued)

Alternative Workshop/ Center Component	Time Frame	Description
Rotation 4	Approximately 15 minutes	Children work in the center/station, and when the bell rings/timer goes off, they clean up and return to the meeting area for another mini-lesson (continued from the previous mini-lesson or on a new topic).
Mini-lesson	2 to 3 minutes	Whole group. The teacher very briefly instructs children on a specific literacy skill/strategy. Children then move to their next center/station.
Rotation 5	Approximately 15 minutes	Children work in the center/station, and when the bell rings/timer goes off, they clean up and return to the meeting area for another mini-lesson (continued from the previous mini-lesson or on a new topic).
Reflect/Share/Closing Meeting	3 to 5 minutes	Teacher/students gather and reflect on and share what they worked on in the centers. The teacher reemphasizes the literacy skills/strategies taught in/across the mini-lessons.

with each lesson either building off the previous one or highlighting a new literacy skill and/or strategy. Students then gather when all rotations are complete for a very brief final share/reflection. In this format, the whole-group instruction seen at the beginning of the standard workshop/centers format is broken into several smaller mini-lessons and spread throughout the rotation.

There are some standard literacy centers/stations that are often included in both workshop/centers formats noted above (see Table 2.3).

Let's take a look at a sample classroom that incorporates responsive play using the standard workshop/centers format (see Figure 2.1). In this first-grade classroom, center rotations include independent reading, partner/small-group reading, writing, listening to reading, word work, and reading with the teacher, as noted in Table 2.1 (Boushey & Moser, 2006).

Children in this classroom use the rug in the library area at the back corner of the room for independent reading; areas of open desk, floor, and carpet space for partner/small-group reading, listening to reading

Table 2.3 Standard Literacy Centers/Stations

Literacy Center	What Is Done in the Center
Independent reading	Children read independently.
Partner/small-group reading	Children sit with a partner/small group and read together. They may read chorally or take turns reading pages.
Writing	Children work on writing, editing, and revising stories/illustrations, poems, letters, and so on.
Listening to reading	Children listen to and read along with audio/digital stories (on computers/tablets, CD players, and so on) individually or with partners/small groups.
Word work	Children work on decoding, spelling, vocabulary, sight words, and so on using games and activities.
Reading with the teacher (This center may rotate along with the others or may be independent of the others for flexibility)	The teacher calls on individual and/or small groups of children to work on various reading skills/strategies and/or uses the time to assess and/or observe students.

Source: Adapted from Boushey & Moser (2006).

(on tablets), and word work; the back kidney-shaped table for writing; and open desks and the student table at the back of the room for word work. The teacher uses the kidney-shaped table near the front of the room to meet with individuals and small groups of students to work on reading and writing skills during the center rotations.

The classroom teacher generally updates center materials each morning before school starts. All materials (other than books for independent and partner/small-group reading, which are generally kept in the classroom library or in individual student book bags) are placed in bins or baskets on a specific shelf in the classroom. When it is time for center rotations, children locate the materials and bring them to the center they will be working in.

After each session (about 15 minutes), the teacher rings a bell, and the students clean up, return the books to the classroom library, and return the materials to the baskets/bins and place them back on the shelf so that they are ready for the next rotation. They then move to the next center (noted by a chart on the wall near the classroom meeting area). The rotations end with a final whole-group meeting (see Table 2.1).

In order to create a *specific* space and time for imaginative and playful literacy learning in this classroom, the teacher *replaced* the partner/

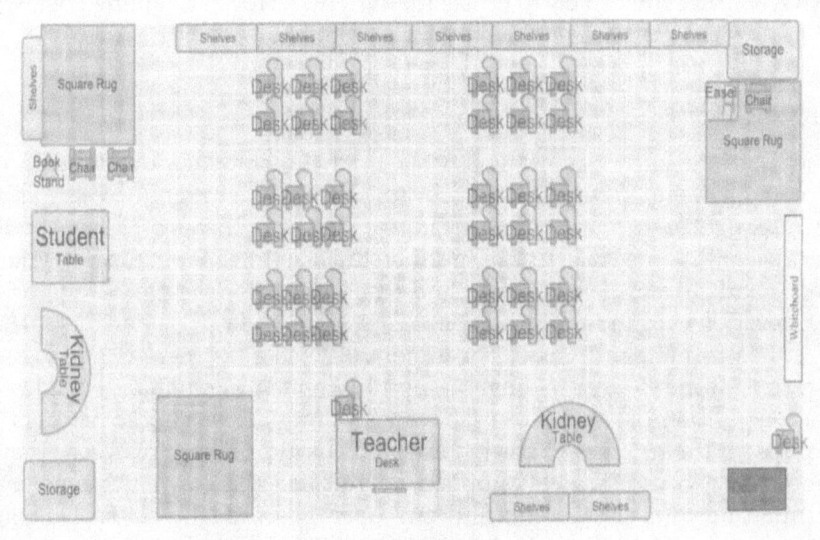

Figure 2.1 **Map of a sample classroom space.** Source: Flint (2016). Created using "Classroom Architect" (ALTEC at the University of Kansas, 2008).

small-group reading center with a responsive play center in her rotations schedule and designated the square carpet (with the easel and chair) in the front corner of the room as the responsive play center space. She also created a basket of carefully chosen books and cutouts to be used in this new center.

For this teacher, replacing the partner/small-group reading center with the responsive play center made sense because the children would still be reading together in small groups or with partners. In your classroom, you may consider this same replacement (which can be made in *either* workshop/centers format), or you might consider adding responsive play as a *new* center in your already established rotations. Your rotations may closely align to one of the formats presented here, or your schedule may look completely different.

You may have enough time built into your daily schedule so that every child can visit five centers *each* day *and* visit with you for small-group instruction. You may only have enough time for the children to rotate through just a few centers each day. Your literacy instruction time might also be split up into several different sections of the school day, or you may not have time for workshop/centers rotations at all. If your schedule or the prescribed curricula do not allow you to implement *any* version of this schedule, you can try to utilize the "anytime" format, outlined below, to implement responsive play in your classroom.

Anytime Format

The anytime format is more flexible than the standard or alternative workshop/centers formats, which follow fairly straightforward and firm sequences. In the anytime arrangement, the entire class, a few small groups, or just one small group/partnership at a time (depending on your needs and capabilities) can read and respond to stories together in various locations around the classroom at any time of day.

In this format, both space and time are flexible, as there is no singular, set classroom area or time-of-day requirement. Essentially, children choose partners or small groups to read with (or you can choose partners/groups for them); choose which books and cutouts or other materials they would like to use (choices supplied by you and placed in a convenient location in your classroom); find any open space in the classroom (on the carpet, at a table, at a group of desks, on the floor) or go to classroom space(s) that you designate; and read, talk, and play together.

In this format, the set time limits and the rotations that are key components of both workshop/centers formats noted above disappear. You can allow children to read and play for a very short amount of time or for as long as you can or want. This way, if you have time at the end of the day, before or after lunch or recess, or after a test, you can implement responsive play quickly, efficiently, and effectively.

Whether you use the standard workshop/centers format, the alternative workshop/centers format, the anytime format, or a format of your own creation, the important thing to remember is that children *need* space, time, materials, and support to meaningfully respond to stories through play in the classroom.

KEY COMPONENTS OF RESPONSIVE PLAY

Beyond providing space(s), time, and materials that invite children to respond to books through play in your classroom, there are other important factors to consider, as noted in the following example.

Collin and Brianna sit on the green carpet in the responsive play center in their first-grade classroom. They look through the three books in the basket and choose to read *Tiger in My Soup* by Kashmira Sheth (2013). This is a story about a boy who desperately wants his sister to read him a book, but she is too distracted, even when he finds a tiger in his soup. As they prepare to play in response to the story, they sort through the sandwich bags of cutouts in the pencil box, find the bag that corresponds to the book they picked, and choose the characters they want to "become."

***

Collin chooses the illustrator cutout (an image of a paintbrush), and Brianna chooses the sister character cutout (an image of the sister from the book). They squish together, elbow to elbow, knee to knee, legs crisscross applesauce, and they lay the book on the floor in front of them. Holding their cutouts, they begin to read together, voices in unison. Collin, *as* the illustrator, swirls the cutout over the pages as they read, "painting" and discussing the details of each picture. Brianna uses the sister character cutout to track the print on the pages and to act out the scenes, bouncing it across the illustrations as they read the words aloud.

They turn the page and see a bowl of soup. Brianna exclaims, "Oh, ABC soup . . . I've had that!" and points to the illustration while Collin begins to sing the alphabet song, "A, B, C, D . . ." Brianna, *as* the sister, begins singing the song with Collin, making the cutout dance across the pages of the book. She then stands up and twirls in a circle, singing quietly and dancing. Collin joins her. They continue reading, talking, playing, singing, dancing, and exploring the story together until they finish the book.

***

As they playfully respond, the children call on their prior knowledge of and their past experiences with alphabet soup, the alphabet song, and their literacy knowledge (knowing their ABCs, their ability to read the story) while engaging with the book *as* the illustrator and *as* the sister from *within* the story. As they read and play together, they also discuss details of the illustrations and practice reading fluently as they chorally (in unison) read each page aloud.

This vignette highlights key components of responsive play. First, the classroom teacher provided space, time, and materials for the children to respond to stories through play. In this case, the classroom had a small green rug that served as a responsive play center. Children were provided with ample time to read together and with materials (cutouts) that invited them to respond through play.

The children were also given autonomy and choice. They were able to choose which book they wanted to read and whether they wanted to use the provided cutouts (and, if so, which ones and how to use them) or not. Importantly, they were also given the freedom to play *if* and *how* they wanted in response to the story. The only real requirements were that the children read together, that they did so relatively quietly, and that they stayed on the carpet.

These key components of responsive play worked together to invite the children to extend their playful reading responses, draw from and build on their prior knowledge, and connect their discussion and play to their literacy learning. Let's further explore these key components of responsive play so that you can determine how to best implement them in your classroom.

Choosing Books and Reading Materials

In the vignette in the beginning of this book, Nathan, Carlos, and Daniel chose to read from a "big book," an oversized book generally used by teachers for group instruction. In the example in this chapter, Collin and Brianna also chose the book they wanted to read together. Three things are important about these examples:

- The *children* chose the books.
- The books were engaging.
- The books elicited playful responses from the children.

When implementing responsive play in your classroom, giving children choices and providing a variety of diverse, engaging, and fun books and reading materials is key. By carefully selecting the books used in your responsive play space(s) and allowing children to choose which books to read, you can support students' literacy development as they read and play together.

Choosing Their Own Books

Imagine that you joined a book club. You arrive, ready to talk about interesting books and to collaboratively choose which one you will read and discuss. But to your surprise, Becky, the book club coordinator, has taken the liberty of choosing the book for the group without any input. Are you still interested in reading the book? Maybe, but maybe not. Thanks a lot, Becky. But would you be *more* interested if you had some say in the choice of book? Probably. Keep this in mind as you provide books in your responsive play space(s) for children to read and respond to.

There should be enough books to give students a choice but not *so* many books that the choice is overwhelming. Providing approximately three books (give or take one or two) for children to choose from is ideal. Book choices will likely be different from day to day or week to week, depending on your classroom learning goals and your responsive play rotation/schedule.

Diverse Books

Chapter 1 shared detailed information about the importance of diverse books, some resources for locating quality diverse children's literature for your classroom library, and lists of diverse books that might pair well with responsive play (see Tables 1.1 to 1.9). This section digs a little deeper into why and how providing access to diverse books can elicit meaningful and playful responses from children, which can lead to literacy learning.

Imagine a classroom where a child searches through book bin after book bin, scouring the shelves, trying to find a book that has a character that looks like them or a book written by an author who writes in the language that they speak at home, but not finding one. Now imagine a classroom where *every* child can see themselves and others in the pages of *various* books in their classroom, where each child can make connections to several authors, characters, and storylines. It's a powerful image—and a significant one.

Children often draw from and demonstrate their experiences and their identities through play in response to storybooks. Responsive play, when paired with a range of books that represent various identities and experiences, can produce pathways through which children can draw from their own experiences and backgrounds to make important connections that inform and support their meaning making and literacy development.

For example, when children see their personal experiences portrayed in stories, they often connect more deeply to the plot—supporting their prediction and comprehension skills. Similarly, when students feel represented by the characters in the storybooks in their classrooms, they often feel more deeply connected to them—supporting their literacy development in relation to analyses of character traits and portrayals. Further, when children read books by authors that they can relate to, they can more readily see *themselves* as authors with something important to say—supporting their reading–writing connections and motivations.

As noted in Chapter 1, beyond acting as mirrors in which children can see themselves, their families, and their communities, diverse books also act as windows and sliding glass doors, allowing children to see, learn about, and become a part of the world(s) of others through stories. This further supports the connections between and among children, story characters, and authors and illustrators.

As you select diverse books for children to choose from during responsive play, be sure to reflect on the classroom you imagined, wherein all students can see themselves and others in various books and can make truly meaningful connections.

"Fun" Books and Reading Materials

Beyond highlighting the need for diverse children's literature in the classroom, Chapter 1 also focused on the importance and value of reading for fun and for joy. This section looks a bit more closely at the types, formats, and genres of books and reading materials that might elicit joyful and playful reading responses in your classroom and why that matters.

Nathan, Carlos, and Daniel chose to read the big book about dogs because of its size. For them, it was fun to read such a giant book! The novelty of it made it appealing to them, along with the fact that they would *all* have to participate in the reading by holding the book, turning the pages, and so on because it was so large. This turned the reading into a team effort, adding to the fun and leading to their playful reading responses.

This example highlights how young children often find ways to utilize play to gain more control over their literacy practices, as a source of pleasure and enjoyment, and as a way to relate and respond to texts in personally significant ways. As they play in response to stories, like the students reading the big book, children can make personal sense of texts as they explore their emotions, their attitudes, and their personal interests, all while having fun.

There are several book and reading material types, formats, and genres that might appeal to the children in your classroom and that can also add to the fun and enjoyment of reading and responding. Using a variety of these will help support children's reading engagement and increase their abilities to make connections to stories and characters, filling the classroom with joy and magic. The types of books you may want to include in your responsive play space(s) broadly include (but are not limited to):

- Picture books
- Easy readers
- Chapter books (possibly)

Keep in mind that picture books and easy readers may be easiest to implement, as chapter books may be too long for children to finish during the time the book is in the responsive play space. But don't be afraid to try using chapter books with your students.

Books and reading materials come in many forms. Your responsive play space(s) should include a variety of these fun and engaging book/reading material formats:

- Board books
- Big books
- Pop-up books
- "I Spy" books
- Comics
- Graphic novels
- Magazines
- Audiobooks
- Digital stories
- Student-authored books and anthologies
- Bilingual and multilingual books

And should include various genres, such as (but not limited to):

- Fiction
- Historical fiction
- Nonfiction
- Biography/autobiography
- Fairy tales/fables
- Folklore/folktales
- Fantasy/science fiction
- Mystery
- Poetry

Variety is the spice of life. Add some jalapeño pepper books to your responsive play menu.

Wordless/Mainly Wordless Picture Books

Beyond the book types, formats, and genres listed above, consider specifically including wordless or mainly wordless picture books in your responsive play space(s). These can be defined as sequenced picture texts or (mainly) wordless narratives in which the reader generally relies on the illustrations to make meaning (Rowe, 1996).

Reading wordless picture books is an open-ended process in which children draw from their own background experiences and knowledge to make sense of the illustrations they encounter in these types of books. Because of their unique format, wordless picture books allow children to construct personal meaning and to create their *own* narratives since there are no (or few) words to explicitly direct their understandings. Children often respond actively and playfully to wordless picture books to construct these meanings and understandings (Flint & Adams, 2018).

As reading wordless/mainly wordless picture books connects visual (illustrations), experiential (children's background knowledge and experiences), print (reading and writing), and affective (feelings, emotions, bodies, movement) dimensions of reading, they support a variety of literacy skills when paired with children's play in the classroom context.

Including these types of books in your responsive play space(s) will support students' language development as they discuss and create their own narratives; literacy development as they use the illustrations and their narratives to make sense of the stories; and social development as they talk, move, play/work, and read together.

Table 2.4 provides a list of some diverse wordless and mainly wordless picture books that might spark imaginative and playful responses from the children in your classroom. Note that this list is not exhaustive. These are just a few of the many wordless and mainly wordless picture books that are available. New and wonderful books are published each year. With the help of your students, you can choose the books that are best suited for responsive play in your classroom.

Table 2.4   Wordless and Mainly Wordless Picture Books

Another by Christian Robinson (2019)
Chalk by Bill Thompson (2010)
Draw! by Raúl Colón (2014)
Drawn Together by Minh Lê, illustrated by Dan Sanat (2018)
Flashlight by Lizi Boyd (2014)
Float by Daniel Miyares (2015)
Flora and the Flamingo by Molly Idle (2013)
Fly by Mark Teague (2019)
Journey by Aaron Becker (2013)
Mirror by Jeannie Baker (2010)
My Friend Rabbit by Eric Rohmann (2002)
No, David! by David Shannon (1998)
Pancakes for Breakfast by Tomie dePaola (2018)
Pool by Jihyeon Lee (2015)
Shine by Dagny Griffin, illustrated by Laura Bobbiesi (2020)
Small in the City by Sydney Smith (2019)
Small Things by Mel Tregonning (2021)
The Arrival by Shaun Tan (2007)
The Lion and the Mouse by Jerry Pinkney (2009)
The Red Book by Barbara Lehman (2004)
The Wanderer by Peter Van den Ende (2020)
Thunderstorm by Arthur Geisert (2013)
Tuesday by David Wiesner (1991)
Wave by Suzy Lee (2008)
Wolf in the Snow by Matthew Cordell (2017)

Note: See "Children's Literature References" in the References section for full citations.

To Read Aloud or Not to Read Aloud? That Is the Question

When choosing books and reading materials to invite children into the world of responsive play, you may wonder if you should read them aloud to the children before they read and respond to them on their own. This is up to you. Keep in mind, though, that research suggests that children benefit *greatly* from opportunities to play out stories during and after listening to read-alouds (Wohlwend, 2023). Hearing stories read aloud can support readers who might find texts challenging and can also aid in deeper comprehension as children reread and play out the stories together after listening to them.

You may find that you read aloud certain books and not others. For example, you might *not* need to read a wordless picture book aloud (though you can) before placing it in your responsive play area, but you might consider reading aloud books that connect to literacy topics that you are teaching in class, that have complex vocabulary words, or that might be generally difficult for most of the students to read on their own.

You may also want to take a "wait-and-see" approach to gauge which books students need more support with as they respond through play. You might choose to read books aloud *before* you place them in the play space, *after* children read and respond to them, or *both*. You know your students and their needs best. Your observations of children as they read and play together will effectively guide your decision making. Keep in mind, though, that read-alouds *do* provide many benefits for your students and that children's play in response to stories that are read aloud can strengthen their story understanding(s) and their retellings.

Guiding Questions for Choosing Books and Reading Materials

You can use the following questions and suggestions to further guide you as you provide books and reading materials for children to choose from in the responsive play spaces in your classroom:

- *Do the books/reading materials reflect a variety of identities?* It is important to provide books and reading materials that reflect multiple identities so that students can see themselves and others in the stories. This will improve reading motivation, engagement, and response.
- *Will the books and reading materials elicit playful responses?* If you see students regularly clamoring to read *Crown: An Ode to the Fresh Cut* by Derrick Barnes (2017) and discussing or acting out barbershop scenes from the story on their own, include it in your responsive play area! Books that are playful and that children already enjoy reading will allow them to respond to stories through talk and play in meaningful ways.

- *Are the books and reading materials at the appropriate "levels"?* Consider placing books in your responsive play space(s) that range in levels of reading difficulty (however you are determining this). Books can be previously read aloud to the class, providing familiarity and easier readability/comprehension as needed (see the previous section).
- *Do the books and reading materials correlate to classroom learning?* Consider including books and reading materials that relate to the content and topics you are discussing in class. For example, when discussing and teaching about sequence of events, provide books that highlight this topic, like *Tuesday* by David Wiesner (1991), a mainly wordless picture book that tells the mysterious tale (in sequence) of frogs that fly through town one Tuesday night. This will help children connect classroom literacy learning with their playful responses.

The "Rules"

Now that you know more about choosing and using books for responsive play, let's talk about the "rules." The first rule of responsive play is that there are no rules for responsive play. Okay, that's not *exactly* true, there are some, but these "rules" are more like guidelines, and these guidelines will be based on your needs and the needs of the students in your classroom.

Often, when adults interfere with or try to direct, control, or take over children's play by making rules, it is no longer the *children's* play. Instead, you should try to plan for, create space and time for, and support children's play in the classroom. The following are some possible guidelines to consider that may help you implement responsive play effectively (in whatever format you choose) without taking over or directing the children's playful responses to stories.

Play

- When implementing responsive play, make sure children know that they *are* allowed to play. Play is often *not* allowed in the classroom, so this is important.
- Do not show or tell children *how* they must play or respond. They will figure out how to play.
- Make sure that children do not feel pressured to play. They should not be *required* to play if they don't want to. If they don't want to play, children can be guided to simply read and discuss books and stories together.

- Sometimes children might get "off task" (not reading, not discussing or playing with a focus on the story, leaving the designated play space). Consider having frequent discussions and/or sessions where you and the children discuss, model, or act out expectations (without directing if/how they should play).

Cutouts/Other Materials

- Make sure that children know that they can use or not use the cutouts or other provided materials as they prefer. These materials should simply be seen as *invitations* for children to play. If the children do not want to use them, they don't have to.
- Do not direct or show children *how* to use cutouts or other materials. Their imaginative play will direct the ways they use them, making the engagements meaningful.
- Ask that children take care of the materials (books, cutouts, toys) so that they don't get lost or ruined.

Books

- Ask that children read the book in full whenever possible. While they may read and play/respond at the same time they read the story or wait to play/respond until after they read the book (either is fine), make sure that they are reading/attempting to read the entire book (if time allows).

Groups/Partners

- The number of children engaged in responsive play will be dictated by your format, as discussed in the "Creating Space(s) and Making Time for Responsive Play" section of this chapter.
  - In the workshop/centers formats, the number of children in groups or partnerships will be guided by how many children are in each station.
  - In the anytime format, you will decide how many children should make up each group or partnership.
  - In either case, consider making groupings and pairings flexible (changing often) so that each child has many opportunities to read and play with other children at various reading "levels" (however you are determining this) and with varying interests, backgrounds, and knowledge.

Working Together

- To prevent problems or arguments, consider having regular discussions about various strategies for solving problems, sharing, and resolving conflicts.
  - Children need opportunities to practice working problems out on their own. Consider giving them the chance to work out any issues themselves before you intervene.

Volume/Noise Level

- Sometimes children's play can be robust and loud.
  - Your workshop/centers rules and guidelines will direct how loud children can and should be in each center.
  - In the anytime format, you may ask children to work at a volume/noise level that you are comfortable with.

Location

- In the workshop/centers formats, ask that students stay in the designated area(s) provided for responsive play (a certain carpet space, table, area on the floor, group of desks) so that they do not disturb other students and so that everyone knows where to go.
- In the anytime format, consider having children choose their own play space(s) and then ask them to stay in that area as they read and play together, or you can designate certain areas for responsive play.

These guidelines will help you encourage the children in your classroom as they read and respond through play in meaningful ways. By being actively involved in planning; creating space(s), time, and materials for play–literacy engagements; and guiding students learning in these ways, you will create a supportive and trusting environment in which responsive play can flourish.

Keep in mind that these are all just *suggested* guidelines; they are not static nor set. You are free to change them, add more personalized guidelines, or take some away. What matters most is that the guidelines work for you and your students.

FINAL THOUGHTS: ADJUSTING RESPONSIVE PLAY TO MEET *YOUR* CLASSROOM NEEDS

This chapter has outlined important aspects of responsive play in the classroom setting, including:

- Space(s), time, and materials
- Choosing books and reading materials
- The "rules"

These components are individually and collectively flexible. Don't be afraid to make them your own. Change the guidelines, make your own "rules," and utilize classroom spaces, times, and materials that make sense for you and your students. Mold responsive play, like Play-Doh, into the shape that best suits your classroom community.

As you implement these components in ways that work for you, be sure that you also build in time for observing the children as they interact with books and with each other and for discussing with them what you notice. By observing, analyzing, and discussing the children's responsive play engagements, you will be better equipped to adjust and modify each of the components to fit your classroom and instructional needs.

Through careful and critical observation, you will also be better able to connect children's playful responses to important literacy skills and strategies that you are working on in class and to assess their literacy learning, as noted in Chapters 3 and 4.

3

Connecting Playful Reader Response to Classroom Literacy Goals

As demonstrated by the parent in the Introduction of this book who was concerned about her child "just playing around with books" and whether this was "really reading," many parents, educators, and administrators might initially view children's play in your classroom as indulgent, unnecessary, and nonacademic. Building on Chapters 1 and 2, this chapter highlights the ways that children's responsive play can be joyous and fun and still connect to classroom literacy goals.

The following sections demonstrate the ways that playful reader response can be leveraged in your classroom as a generative and meaningful source of academic learning. The chapter concludes with some final thoughts on how and why it can also be important to *(re)play* reading responses with children, emphasizing critical aspects of their playful responses to stories.

CONNECTING TO PERSONAL EXPERIENCES AND KNOWLEDGE

The responsive play framework suggests that children respond to literature and to each other through their play by connecting their personal lives, experiences, and knowledge to the books they read together. In the following vignette, Logan, Diego, and Daniella read and playfully respond to *Thunderstorm*, a mainly wordless picture book by Arthur Geisert (2013) that portrays a farm at different stages during a destructive storm. The children draw from their personal knowledge and experiences to inform their responses to the book and make connections to the story and each other.

***

Logan chooses a mirror cutout and announces that he is "the reader." Diego holds up a cutout that depicts an image of a tornado from the story and says, "I'm this!" Daniella chooses the cutout with an image of a sheep.

Logan begins to narrate the story. "Once upon a time there was a storm ... and there was three piggies' houses," pointing to the illustration of the farmhouse and barn. Logan turns the page, looks at the illustrations, and says, "It's raining!" Daniella bounces her sheep cutout across the pages and in a sheepish voice says, "It's a rainstorm!" Diego shouts, "It's me! I'm the tornado!" and swirls his cutout over the illustration.

Surprised at an illustration, Diego then says, "Woah, that's water!" Following up, Daniella suggests, "This world, it had water floods . . . from the ocean." Logan agrees and says that when he was in California, he saw a "humongous flood." Diego asks, "Floods?" and tilts his head, looking at Logan (he is unsure of the meaning of the word). Logan nods and says, "It covered my tent!" and gestures with his hand above his head. Diego seems to understand what Logan and Daniella mean by the word "flood" and says, "It was all water, huh?! Sploooosh!" (he waves his hand over the illustration). Both Daniella and Logan nod and say, "Yah!"

***

Studies of children's responses to storybooks reveal how children's reading work and play intertwine and become one as they construct meaning and respond to stories together in the classroom (Pantaleo, 2008). Meaning making is significantly influenced by children's personal knowledge and experiences as well as by classroom literacy practices. Accordingly, the children in this vignette draw from and share their own knowledge and personal experiences, through responsive play and discussion, to make sense of the story in relation to their own worlds.

Here, as the reader, Logan retells the story in his own words. Drawing on his previous reading experiences, he uses his knowledge of traditional storybook language and begins with "Once upon a time." He also interweaves the story with the tale *The Three Little Pigs* (discussed more in the following "Intertextuality" section). Next, Daniella describes her knowledge of a flood that happened in real life, likely referring to a tsunami or hurricane. Logan then relates to Daniella's shared knowledge as he tells his own story about a flood that he personally witnessed in California while on a camping trip.

The thunderstorm and tornado in the story brought great destruction to the farm. Daniella's personal knowledge of flooding prompts discussion and informs the group's meaning making in relation to the destructive forces of nature and the storm depicted within the book. This allows Logan to then share his own personal experiences with flooding and to connect with Daniella and to the story.

In turn, this playful interaction and the sharing of personal knowledge and experiences allows Diego, who is learning English, to understand the meaning of the word "flood." To sum up his newfound knowledge, Diego uses responsive play to demonstrate his understanding by washing over the illustration with a mighty "sploooosh!" as he playfully becomes an imagined wave, washing over the story landscape.

Discussion

Reading often involves focusing on the "lived-through" experiences of a story (Rosenblatt, 1978). This focus allows readers to have a virtual experience in which they become a part of and "live" within the story world, connect with characters, and become emotionally invested in the story (Galda & Liang, 2003). By connecting their prior knowledge and experiences to the information presented within the book and to the others they are sharing the reading and play experience with, the children in this vignette build their knowledge and facilitate their own meaning making and learning.

It is exactly these sorts of meaningful experiences that allow children to make *further* connections in the academic context (Dewey, 1938). Through their reading, play, and discussions, language and literacy learning are supported and expanded in the classroom setting.

INTERTEXTUALITY

Intertextuality is defined as the knowledge and experiences children draw on, from varied sources, to expand their knowledge, construct meaning, make connections to stories and each other, and respond to books in various ways. Children's responses to literature often reflect their abilities to relate the story being read to other meaningful cultural texts and products, including other books and stories, media and popular culture, and classroom learning.

In the following examples, informed and guided by their intertextual knowledge, children connect previous literacy and learning experiences with stories and with each other and transform these into imaginative and playful responses.

Other Books and Stories

As they transact with each other and with stories, children often relate *other* books to the stories they are reading, informing their responsive play and their understandings. For example, in the vignette highlighted in the "Connecting to Personal Experiences and Knowledge" section above, when the children read *Thunderstorm*, Logan draws from his previous home and school storybook reading experiences and uses traditional fairy-tale language as he begins the retelling with "Once upon a time," taking on a narrator or storyteller role.

Logan also suggests that the story he is telling, as the imagined narrator, is similar to (or *is*) the story *The Three Little Pigs*. He draws from this well-known (to him) tale to imaginatively reinterpret the story and illustrations in *Thunderstorm*. He references and points to illustrations in the *Thunderstorm* book as he describes and retells portions of the tale, connecting and intertwining the two stories in creative and playfully responsive ways.

In a similar example, Mateo, Paige, and Lucia read *Tuesday* (the wordless picture book that highlights flying frogs).

***

Using a frog character cutout, Paige becomes a frog and flies away from Lucia, who has become the dog that chases the frogs in the illustration. As they play and chase each other with the cutouts, Mateo shouts, "You can't catch me, I'm the Gingerbread Man!"

***

Prompted by the flight of the frogs in the book and the way that they follow the dog in the illustration, the children playfully chase each other with the cutouts as they become these characters within the story. During their responsive play, Mateo draws from his knowledge of other books as he playfully suggests, "You can't catch me, I'm the Gingerbread Man!" Here, Mateo draws on his intertextual story knowledge of *The Gingerbread Man* (a story in which a gingerbread man runs away from various characters) to inform his interpretations of the *Tuesday* book and to creatively and imaginatively inform the play that the children are engaged in.

Past experiences with literature are important aspects of children's histories that they bring with them to classroom literacy events in order to "live through" reading experiences, make meaningful connections, and play with(in) stories. As such, the ways that children draw from other books to inform their readings and responses can create opportunities to bring stories to life and infuse them with meaning and context, creating connections that inform and impact their understandings and their learning in your classroom.

Media and Popular Culture

Just as children connect stories to other books they have read in the past, children also make important and meaningful connections to popular culture. In the following vignettes, children demonstrate the ways that media and pop culture inform their playful responses to stories.

Movies, Superheroes, and Princesses

Cody, Tuan, and Noah flip through the pages of the *Tuesday* book and laugh at the illustrations of the frogs flying around the town. They quickly read through the book and then decide who to "become" as they plan their play.

Cody holds up a frog character cutout and moves it across the pages, suggesting that he is "flying around." They continue flipping through the pages of the book and using the frog cutouts to fly across and through the illustrations on each page. Noah chooses to become the reader and narrates the story as they continue to flip through the pages.

Cody, looking at the illustration that shows several frogs in the air, says, "They're invading like aliens! Men in Black!" Noah turns more pages and continues narrating the events. After seeing the illustration in which a frog wears a sheet as a cape, Cody suggests that he is "like Superman" and shouts, "Superfrog to the rescue!" Tuan reiterates that the frogs are "invading" and moves his cutout swiftly across the pages.

***

Here, the children reference the fact that the frogs seem to be "invading" the town and suggest that they are space aliens. Drawing from his knowledge of movies, Cody shouts, "Men in Black!," referencing the popular movie about aliens on Earth. The children, prompted by the illustration in the book of a frog in a cape, also reference their media and pop-culture knowledge, this time in regard to superheroes. Because the frog wears a cape, he takes on the persona of "Superfrog," like Superman, in the eyes of the children.

These media and pop-culture references inform the children's actions as they read the book and respond through play. In another vignette discussed later in this chapter, Julieta also suggests, "Hey, everybody . . . we have a superhero!" as she reads the *Tuesday* book with Marianna.

Similar to superhero play, children also engage in princess play.

***

As Paige and Alyssa read the *Thunderstorm* book together, Alyssa holds up the reader cutout (with an image of a mirror) and says, "Mirror, mirror, on the wall ... who is the fairest of them all?!" connecting the responsive play to the *Snow White* movie. Alyssa happily responds, "Paige is ... Paige is the princess!"

***

Young children's incorporation of superhero and princess narratives in their play and in their writing has been explored in many capacities (Dyson, 1994; Marsh, 2000; Paley, 1984). This type of play is attractive to children, who often use it to explore autonomy and agency as they position themselves as important people and heroes within the play context (Marsh, 2000).

Here, the children draw from their intertextual pop-culture knowledge in relation to movies, superheroes, and princesses as they construct meaning and understanding through their responsive play. Making these types of connections and trying on these different identities is important for children in that, as they make "use of popular and traditional cultural symbols (like Superman or Cinderella)" (Dyson, 1996, p. 472), they playfully position themselves within stories in ways that allow them to critically reflect on characters and storylines that highlight dominant cultural narratives.

Classroom Learning

Children not only draw from their knowledge of other books, media, and popular culture but also rely on their intertextual knowledge related to school. They draw from experiences and educational content found within the classroom to inform their responsive play. In the following vignettes, children connect their playful responses to their learning across content areas.

Let's revisit the vignette in the "Key Components of Responsive Play" section of Chapter 2, wherein Collin and Brianna read *Tiger in My Soup* together. This is the story about a boy who desperately wants his sister to read him a book, but she is too distracted, even when he finds a tiger in his soup.

***

As the sister, Brianna exclaims, "Oh, ABC soup . . . I've had that!" and points to the illustration while Collin begins to sing the alphabet song. The two sing the ABC song and dance and twirl together.

***

Informed by her experience with and her knowledge of the type of soup in the illustration, Brianna suggests that it is ABC soup (it has noodles in the shapes of letters). Collin then sings the alphabet song (the ABCs) as he paints the image of the soup and the letters onto the page. Brianna joins in, and they playfully read, sing, and paint together.

Students often practice their ABCs as preschoolers and kindergartners and at the beginning of the first-grade school year by singing the alphabet song and by reviewing letters and letter sounds. Collin and Brianna call on their knowledge of and experience with the ABCs as well as their knowledge of classroom and home experiences with the alphabet while they sing the song together. This connects their prior experiences with literacy instruction to the text and directly informs their responsive play.

In another example, Bianca and Kaylee read *Thunderstorm* together and draw from their classroom learning to inform their playful responses to the book. In the story, a clock is prominently featured to note the time passing and the time of each event in relation to the storm.

***

As they plan their responsive play, Bianca suggests that she will be the clock in the story. "You're gonna be the clock?!" Kaylee asks. "Yah!" Bianca says as she puts her arms in the air and moves them like clock hands. "Tick, tock, tick, tock," she says as she moves her arms. Kaylee then notes, "Actually, I know how to be a clock! Like our teacher showed us!" Bianca nods and smiles and says, "I know!" Both girls then stand up and become the clocks on each of the pages, matching the times with their arms.

***

In class, Bianca and Kaylee learned how to use their arms like clock hands on an analog clock to demonstrate different times. Through their play in response to the book, Bianca and Kaylee draw from this lesson to "become" the clock in the story, connecting their classroom learning to the story and to their responsive play.

Reading and responding to books together, the children in these vignettes connected their classroom learning to their reading transactions, informing their responsive play in intertextual ways.

Discussion

The children in these examples draw from and build upon their personal experiences and intertextual knowledge to inform their responses to stories, build understanding(s), and create connections in relation to:

- Other books and stories
- Media and pop culture
- Classroom learning

When combined in a classroom context, as noted in the vignettes seen here, children's shared readings produce pathways through which they can draw from their intertextual knowledge to simultaneously inform their literacy learning and their play. By integrating cooperative literacy events with their own life experiences and personal knowledge in the classroom context and then translating these into playful reactions to literature through responsive play, children can actively construct meaning together.

DEVELOPING AND PRACTICING LITERACY SKILLS AND STRATEGIES

Beyond drawing from and building on their personal experiences and intertextual knowledge through imaginative play, children can also develop and practice other important skills. This portion of the chapter highlights the ways that children's responsive play can be fun and still connect *directly* to specific classroom literacy skills, strategies, standards, and learning goals.

This is important. As mentioned in the opening of this chapter, in today's often restrictive academic climate, play may be seen as nonacademic and thus not generally allowed in your classroom. If you can demonstrate that children are practicing and developing important language and literacy skills through their play in meaningful ways, administrators and parents will be better able to recognize responsive play's value in the classroom context.

The sections below highlight the ways that children demonstrate their abilities to retell and extend stories, work and play with words, make story predictions, enhance their comprehension, analyze stories, reflect critically, and view books as meaningful artifacts.

Retelling Stories

In the following vignette, Julieta and Mariana read *Tuesday* together. Here, they collectively retell the story as they play. Using character cutouts, Julieta becomes a frog, and Mariana initially becomes a frog and later becomes the dog in the story.

***

Julieta says, "I'm a frog . . . I'm flyinnnggggg! There's a house, everyone!" Mariana props the book open so they can read the book and use the cutouts at the same time. Retelling the story, Julieta says, "My brother's hanging on the rope! Hey, everybody . . . we have a superhero!," referring to the image of a frog in the cape. Mariana turns the page, looks at the illustration that shows a frog changing the channel with his tongue, and says, "Find the Grammy! How 'bout we change this channel, this isn't good to watch."

Julieta, following the sequence of events in the illustrations, then says, "We have to fly away from the dog, everybody!" Mariana replies as the dog, "Wait, we're not scared of you now, giddyup!," and Julieta laughs. Turning another page, Mariana says, "Ahhh! We're off our lily pads! We have to do something before everybody falls!," and Julieta replies, "We're falling into the water! Retreat, retreat!" Mariana, noting an image of a detective in the story who is trying to determine what has happened, says, "I wanna be that guy." Julieta, looking at the final illustrations in the story, says, "We can't believe it . . . we were flying!"

***

As they become characters and reenact and retell the story in their own words, these children demonstrate their comprehension of the book's plot. They expertly (re)interpret the storyline and make sense of the characters and their actions and then demonstrate them through their responsive play. When children read and explore book themes and characters together and retell stories in their own words in these ways, new potentials for meaning construction are created (Rowe, 1998).

Story Making: Transforming and Extending Stories

Within their retellings, when they revisit characters and play out story scenes, children often transform, extend, and create new stories through their responsive play. In this example, Alyssa and Maya read *Creepy*

Carrots by Reynolds (2012). In this story, a rabbit who loves to eat carrots begins to be mysteriously followed by them.

***

After reading the story, as they prepare to play in response, Alyssa says, "Wait . . . the end will *really* be that they were camping and then they saw the creepy carrots . . . and he gets revenge, and his revenge was to eat them!" Maya laughs and says, "Yah! Revenge!" and uses the rabbit cutout to eat the carrot cutout. "Chomp!" Both Alyssa and Maya laugh.

***

Responsive play allows children to imagine and play with and through books together. Children can cooperatively build on, construct, and re-create their understandings of characters and stories, become those characters, and live with(in) the stories as they make sense of them.

In this vignette, responsive play allows the children to enter the story world, join the story experiences, and demonstrate their understanding of the characters and their comprehension of the story. Alyssa and Maya then share a creative (re)interpretation of the story as they discuss and play out an *alternate* ending wherein the rabbit, realizing he was tricked by the creepy carrots into never going near them again, gets revenge and eats them all. Through their imaginative story making, the children *extend* the storyline, elaborate on it, and create new scenarios for the reimagined character, highlighting important literacy skills.

Working and Playing with Words

Children also demonstrate important literacy skills as they focus on the *words* within the stories as they read and play. In this vignette, Paige, Lucia, and Mia read *Creepy Carrots* and figure out a hard-to-read word together.

***

Paige chooses a character cutout and announces that she is a carrot. Lucia also chooses a carrot cutout and shows Paige, "I'm this creepy carrot!" Mia notes that she is "the reader" and opens the book: "I'll read the words!" As she reads, Paige and Lucia use the cutouts to act out the scenes on each page.

Mia then lets Paige join her as the reader because Paige exchanges her carrot cutout for a reader cutout. Paige reads, "After . . ." and then pauses and points to a word on the page and looks to Mia for help. Mia points to each letter in the word, sounding out each letter as she points, "J . . . a . . . s . . . per." Paige shouts, "Jasper!" and continues reading.

***

When Paige is unable to read a word, she looks to Mia, as the other reader, for help. Mia supports Paige in the reading process by pointing to each letter and pronouncing the sounds so that Paige can effectively read the word for herself.

This type of peer support, as a way to help each other figure out difficult words, is often seen when children read and play together. The social nature of the children's responsive play allows them to practice various strategies and skills they have learned in class in meaningful ways and ultimately enhances their literacy learning as they support each other's reading.

Making Predictions

Children often make predictions about what might happen next in a story. This is an important literacy skill that aids in comprehension. In the following vignette, Hunter and Carlos read *The Paper Bag Princess* by Munsch (1980). This is a story in which traditional gender roles are reversed and the princess saves herself and the prince from a dragon by using her wit.

***

Hunter becomes the reader and begins to read the story. Carlos becomes the dragon, shouting "Rawwwr!" as he moves his cutout across the page. Carlos suggests, "Now I think she's gonna say, I'm NOT marrying him!" Hunter, now acting as the illustrator, agrees and points to the page, "Yah, she won't . . . 'cause look . . . I drew her like she doesn't like him."

***

Carlos predicts that the princess in the story will say that she will not marry the prince. Taking on the illustrator role, Hunter "draws" the princess character in the illustration and suggests that Carlos is correct, as he imaginatively draws the character to look like she does not like the prince, corroborating this prediction.

Becoming characters and participating in story worlds, children take on active roles as they make predictions and construct meaning together while they play in response to stories (Pantaleo, 2008). Making predictions in these ways helps children think about stories and sequences of events as they create understandings together, ultimately building their comprehension of the story and of the characters and their motivations.

Building Comprehension: Clarifying Understandings and Meanings

In the vignette in the "Working and Playing with Words" section above, Paige, Lucia, and Mia read *Creepy Carrots* and figure out a hard-to-read word together. Here, they continue to read and play in order to clarify meanings and further build their story comprehension.

***

As they play out the story scenes together, Paige looks at an illustration with a headstone that says "R.I.P." and asks, "Wait . . . what *is* this part?" Lucia points to the picture and says, "OK, this is . . . Rest in Peace." Paige points to each letter and says, "So, Rest . . . in . . . Peace." Lucia nods, and Paige follows up, "You told me that before." Lucia is surprised and says, "Really?" Paige reminds her that she told her on Halloween when they read another book together that had similar headstones.

***

Here, Paige seeks clarification on something she sees in an illustration and asks what R.I.P. means on the depicted headstones. Lucia knows this information, draws on her previous knowledge, and shares it with Paige to help her to construct an understanding of the abbreviation. As they play together and reinterpret the story, their knowledge is cooperatively shared in order to enhance comprehension.

Similarly, when Alyssa, Carlos, and Hunter read the *Tuesday* book, they collaboratively construct their understandings of the story events.

***

Alyssa becomes the illustrator and paints the images on each page as Carlos and Hunter retell the story in their own words and play out the scenes. Carlos, as a frog, points to an illustration depicting a detective who is examining the lily pads dropped throughout the town and says, "Who's this guy?" Hunter replies, "Probably a detective trying to solve floating frogs . . . !" and floats his hand over and across the page.

***

As they play, Carlos attempts to clarify story information to improve his understanding of what's happening. Hunter suggests that the character Carlos is asking about is probably a detective trying to solve the case of the mysterious floating frogs, demonstrating his intertextual knowledge, as he has likely seen detective characters in other stories or TV shows.

He shares this knowledge with Carlos, simultaneously demonstrating his understanding of the story and supporting Carlos's comprehension of the story events. This helps Carlos to clarify his understanding and construct story meaning. Hunter then pretends that his hand is a frog that floats mysteriously out of the pages, extending his explanation and rejoining the responsive play.

As the children in these vignettes play with(in) and through the stories, they share knowledge to create meanings and understandings together, build on and practice important literacy skills, and support each other's comprehension of story components and events in purposeful and meaningful ways.

Analyzing Stories: Story Structure and Sequence of Events

While reworking, retelling, and re-creating stories through their play, children also practice literacy skills by analyzing stories and their features. In this vignette, Julieta and Mariana analyze the story structure of *Tuesday* as they prepare to reinterpret it through play.

***

Julieta says, "K, let's act it out!" Agreeing, Mariana says, "How 'bout we make it from first, next, then last?" Julieta agrees and says, "First, the guy with the sandwich." Mariana disagrees and flips through the book: "No, first the frogs." Julieta then suggests they use the cutouts to put the story in order of the events shown in the illustrations.

"First, second . . . last, pigs!" Julieta says, laughing. They place the cutouts in the order of the events that occur in the story. They then retell the story from the beginning and act out each scene, using the ordered cutouts as a guide.

***

Through their "out-of-play talk," Julieta and Mariana propose new ideas as they plan their play in response to the story. This type of talk allows them to clarify and demonstrate their understandings of story structure and their comprehension of the story in relation to the sequence of events (Sawyer & DeZutter, 2017). Talk of this sort is directly related to story recall, story reproduction, and story comprehension. Here, the children use this type of talk to inform their responsive play, which simultaneously draws from and informs their recall and understanding of the story.

Reflecting Critically

As critical readers of texts, children not only construct understandings by analyzing story structures but also demonstrate great depth in their analyses of characters as they are depicted in stories and illustrations and in the ways that they portray these characters through their responsive play.

Characters and Gender Roles

Reading *Tiger in My Soup*, Julieta and Mariana settle in to read the story together and choose the cutouts they would like to become as they prepare to play in response to the book.

***

"I'm gonna be the sister," Marianna says excitedly. Julieta replies, "K. I'm gonna be the boy." Marianna looks at the illustration and says, "I'm pouring you soup!" Julietta says, "Mmmm" in a low voice as she eats the soup.

***

"Children are active and powerful players in the classroom as they talk and interact with gender discourses and each other" (Blaise, 2005, p. 24). In this brief vignette, Julietta and Marianna draw from their understandings of what it means to "be a girl" and what it means to "be a boy" (Wohlwend, 2012) as they actively perform gender through their responsive play, though in simplistic ways, as seen when Julietta lowers her voice as she becomes "the boy."

Here, it is considered appropriate and acceptable for the girls to perform both female and male roles as they playfully respond to the story. Importantly, as they play with(in) the story in this way, they also negotiate, create, and re-create their understandings of identity, gender, and gender roles in relation to storybook characters (Flint, 2020a).

Relating to stories and characters through their play in this way, the children interweave their experiences and their knowledge with their playful reading transactions to explore different perspectives. They also take on active roles as they negotiate various gendered identities and, as seen in the girls' willingness to play male roles, challenge dominant gender norms (Davies & Banks, 1992; Dutro, 2003).

Viewing Books as Meaningful Artifacts

Beyond inserting themselves into stories, analyzing story components, and reflecting critically about characters, children also construct their understandings of books as *objects* as they play in response to stories. In the vignette below, Bianca, Kaylee, and Brianna read *Tuesday* together.

***

Searching through the cutouts, Bianca says, "I write the words. No . . . I read, I'm the reader." Kaylee says, "Illustrator! I love to draw pictures!" and chooses the illustrator cutout. Brianna then says, "Okay, I will be the author." Kaylee follows up and says, "We're making the book!"

***

The children in this vignette choose character cutouts in order to respond to the story and begin to playfully *create* the book. In becoming the reader, illustrator, and author, the children take on differing points of view in relation to the book as an *object*. While they are "making the book," as Kaylee suggests, they are also constructing an understanding of books as products and "artifacts," which, according to Pahl and Rowsell (2010, p. 2):

- Have physical features that make them distinct;
- Are created objects that use and evoke language;
- Embody people, stories, thoughts, communities, identities, and experiences; and
- Are valued and made by meaning makers in particular contexts.

The children in this vignette repurpose the book and the story as an artifact and create a scenario in which they can respond to the different aspects and features of the book itself. Rather than focusing on the storyline, the events, or the characters in the story, they take on the roles of the book *creators* within their responsive play. In this context, the book and the story have very different purposes than they would if the children chose to play character roles and retell the story, as seen in other vignettes.

Their responsive play, in this regard, demonstrates their understanding that just as the printed words and illustrations inside of the books have meaning and tell stories, so do the book creators—and the books themselves.

Discussion

When children reinterpret stories through playful responses and repurpose books through imaginative play, knowledge is built upon, and meaning is ultimately constructed. The sections above highlight the ways that responsive play can connect directly to literacy learning goals and allow children to meaningfully demonstrate their abilities to:

- Retell stories
- Read difficult words
- Make informed predictions
- Comprehend and analyze story components and features
- Reflect critically on important ideas and topics
- View books as meaningful artifacts

In turn, these demonstrations of skill and strategy practice and literacy learning can help you make the case for responsive play in your classroom.

FINAL THOUGHTS: (RE)PLAYING

This chapter has outlined the ways that children's responsive play can connect directly to your classroom literacy goals. Various stories and vignettes were shared to demonstrate how playful reader response can be used in your classroom as a meaningful source of learning, including:

- Connecting to personal experiences and knowledge
- Intertextuality
- Developing and practicing literacy skills and strategies

Keep these examples in mind as you begin your journey into playful reader response and as you share your own stories of success with parents and administrators throughout your playful adventure. Also keep in mind that, beyond supporting children's literacy learning in the ways noted above, the types of conversations and character analyses demonstrated by children, brought about by meaningful engagements with books and with each other through play, can also open doors for *critical conversations* in your classroom. Including responsive play in your instruction can allow you to interact with students during and after their playful responses and engage in critical questioning and conversations about important topics and concepts.

Play scenarios can be discussed and possibly *(re)played*, allowing children to talk about various aspects of dominant cultural and classroom norms and to discuss ways they can challenge stereotypes through their playful portrayals. For example, responsive play can allow you and your students to discuss and challenge gendered assumptions, such as gender roles and the gender binary, as seen in the vignette wherein Julieta takes on a male role during her playful response.

In this example, you could guide students to (re)play the story, with various children taking on different roles (such as males playing female roles and vice versa) as they become the characters, and then discuss the portrayals and the implications of these. Here, discussions and (re)playings could center on gender(ed) stereotypes of storybook characters and why these are important to notice and to talk about.

When children engage with books in critical ways, discussing and (re)playing important issues like gender and race, they can "reimagine where they stand in the world—and in stories"—and raise their own voices for equity in the classroom context (Enciso, 2021, p. 102). Correspondingly, it is important that you make and take the time to observe your students' responsive play to capitalize on opportunities like these for critical conversations in your classroom. In the next chapter, you will be guided to consider various ways of observing and assessing your student's learning as they play with(in) and through stories.

4

✣

Observing, Documenting, and Assessing Literacy Learning

Research on young children's meaning making suggests that stories provide a major pathway to understanding (Wells, 1986). As seen throughout this book, children negotiate and construct meaning through their imaginary play with books in the classroom. Children merge their transactions with stories with their own experiences and knowledge and transform these into playful and meaningful literary responses. Responsive play, in this regard, affords children important opportunities for literacy learning and meaning making in the classroom context.

As noted in the vignettes highlighted in Chapters 2 and 3, children demonstrate their sophisticated thinking about complex concepts and topics through their play. Children's play in response to stories encourages their use of interpretive strategies and suggests that they move *beyond* simple comprehension and recall of story events into *deeper* interpretations and understandings of stories and characters when they respond through play (Rowe, 2007).

These vignettes demonstrate, in various ways, how children's play, language, and literacy are complementary; that children's responsive play should be encouraged in the classroom setting; and that children's experiences and funds of knowledge should be valued as *additive* to the academic learning context.

At this point in the book, you're likely (hopefully) thinking, "Okay, this all sounds awesome, but how do I document and assess my students' learning as they engage in responsive play?" Great question. You will probably need to *show* parents and administrators that your students are, in fact, learning as they play with(in) books in order to successfully continue your responsive play journey together.

Building on Chapter 3, this chapter will guide you to consider ways of observing and documenting children's literacy learning as they play with(in) books. The sections below will define and discuss *kidwatching* and *playwatching* and share details about how to combine and implement these in your classroom through a *responsive playwatching* framework. Next, you will find valuable information about and resources for documenting children's knowledge, assessing their learning, and building on their experiences to create meaningful literacy instruction. This chapter concludes with some final thoughts on self-evaluation.

OBSERVING CHILDREN'S PLAY

Kidwatching

Kidwatching is a way to get to know students and to inform instructional practices through careful and critical observation. Essentially, kidwatching includes (Owocki & Goodman, 2002):

- Observing and taking note of what students know and can do
- Trying to understand how students construct and express their knowledge
- Reflecting on observations and instruction

Doing these things will allow you to:

- Organize a rich learning environment
- Observe and document children's knowledge
- Analyze data

Together, all these components will help you to shape your classroom literacy instruction.

Playwatching

Playwatching is a more specific form of kidwatching that intentionally focuses on observing the ways that children engage with and interact with others and/or with materials as they play (Wohlwend, 2013a). This type of kidwatching is more than just systematic observation. It is also

> valuing the contributions each child makes within the learning community that is our classroom. It is helping children realize who is an expert at what

and who they can turn to when they need assistance. It is giving voice to students who might otherwise be silent. It is getting to know each child in as many contexts as possible—to know each child as a person unique in all the world. (O'Keefe, 1997, p. 5, as cited in Wohlwend, 2013a)

Playwatching can allow teachers to observe and analyze children's play in relation to their learning and development in the classroom. Importantly, it also positions children as knowledgeable and unique and frames their ways of knowing (including their play) as informative to classroom learning objectives and instruction.

Responsive Playwatching

In order to construct detailed knowledge about the ways in which your students expertly integrate play and literacy in your classroom, you can use responsive playwatching. This *combines* kidwatching and playwatching into one framework. This framework supports classroom data collection that is systematic, personalized, and focused on the valuable knowledge and experiences of each student—based on your observations of their conversations, interactions, and playful responses to stories.

DOCUMENTING CHILDREN'S ENGAGEMENTS

Observation and documentation go hand in hand. The main focus of observing the children in your classroom through responsive playwatching is to document what they know and how they express this knowledge through their play with(in) and through books. There are a variety of ways that you can document children's responsive play in your classroom:

- *Responsive play checklists*—These checklists are a quick and simple way to determine what your students know and how they demonstrate what they know while engaging in responsive play. These checklists can tie to literacy goals and standards and include skills and strategies related to phonemic awareness, phonics, fluency, vocabulary, comprehension, and personal knowledge and experiences. What is on these checklists will be different depending on the time of year and what you are looking for. They can be used to track student learning and development over time.
- *Responsive play anecdotal records*—These are quick notes that briefly describe what the children are doing and saying as you observe their responsive play. These can be written on sticky notes (organized how you prefer), on blank sheets of paper (one page per child, orga-

nized how you prefer), in a journal or notebook, or on a sheet/form that has all your students' names on it, each in their own box.
- For example, in one box, you can note, *3/5/2024—Dahlia and Tianna read* Goodnight Moon. *Tianna becomes the reader and helps Dahlia read the word "goodnight" by saying that two o's make the "oo" sound but that it's different from the sound in "moon"* (see Table 4.1).
- *Detailed responsive play notes*—These can be used when you have more time to observe children's responsive play. These notes will be more detailed than the anecdotal records and may look more like a transcript, with direct quotes. Like anecdotal records, these can be taken in a journal/notebook or on a sheet of paper but will require more space than the limited boxes found on the responsive play anecdotal records sheet.
  - For example, if the anecdotal record above was written instead as detailed responsive play notes, it may look more like what is shown here:

March 5, 2024

Dahlia and Tianna read Goodnight Moon *together in the classroom library, on the carpet.*

Tianna: I want to be the reader! (picks up the book)

Dahlia: I'm the mom bunny! (chooses the character cutout with the adult bunny on it). But I wanna read too!

Tianna and Dahlia begin to read together (chorally), and Dahlia acts out the scenes on the pages as the bunny character.

Dahlia: (looks at Tianna because she doesn't know how to read the word "goodnight")

Tianna: (pointing to the "oo" in the word) It says "oo," so it's different than "moon" (pointing to the word "moon").

Dahlia: Oh yah!

They continue to read and act out the scenes together.

To help you observe and document your students' playful responses to stories, consider using the following:

- *Responsive playwatching form*—This form combines aspects of the responsive play checklists, responsive play anecdotal records, and detailed responsive play notes highlighted above. The responsive

Observing, Documenting, and Assessing Literacy Learning 59

Table 4.1 Responsive Play Anecdotal Records Sheet

Student Name	Student Name	Student Name	Student Name
Student Name	Student Name	Student Name	Student Name
Student Name	Student Name	Student Name	Student Name
Student Name	Student Name	Student Name	Student Name
Student Name	Tianna 3/5/2024—Dahlia and Tianna read Goodnight Moon. *Tianna becomes the reader and helps Dahlia read the word "goodnight" by saying that two o's make the "oo" sound but that it's different from the sound in "moon."*	Student Name	Student Name

Source: Adapted from Owocki & Goodman (2002).

playwatching form has space for the student's name, the date, and the book they are reading at the top. It also has boxes with key aspects of responsive play that you should watch for (like a checklist) and ample space next to these for extended anecdotal records and reflections. It also has space at the bottom of the form for more detailed notes, along with your thoughts on what you noticed (see Table 4.2).

Table 4.2 Responsive Playwatching Form

Student Name: _____
Date Observed: _____
Book(s) Used: _____

What to Look For	Examples and Instances
Practicing reading, fluency	
Making personal connections: Knowledge and/or experiences	
Making intertextual connections: Other books, media, pop culture, classroom learning	
Retelling stories	
Transforming or extending stories	
Working with words (phonemic awareness, phonics, word building, figuring out unknown words, strategy use)	
Making predictions	

(Continued)

Table 4.2 (Continued)

Comprehension	
Story structure and/or sequence of events	
Character analysis	
Critical reflections (race, gender, language)	
Books as artifacts	
Other (joy/fun, language skills, social skills)	

Notes: _____

_____
_____
_____
_____
_____
_____
_____
_____
_____
_____
_____
_____
_____
_____
_____

Source: Adapted from Flint (2016).

You can also collect other forms of responsive play documentation in your classroom, including:

- Book lists (lists of books children have read and responded to through play)
  - Book genre/style preferences of children
- Writings children have done as extensions of or connections to their responsive play (we will talk more about writing in Chapter 5)
- Notes on children's language use during responsive play (words used, vocabulary)
- Examples (notes, transcripts) of children's story retellings
- Notes on children's self-evaluations (discussed later in this chapter)

As you prepare and plan to observe your students as they engage in responsive play, you can schedule dates and times that are convenient for you to take these notes, making sure each student gets observed multiple times. Consider using file folders or binders to store your records for each student in a way that makes sense for you. This important documentation can help you show parents and administrators the value of responsive play for your students' literacy learning and development over the school year.

ASSESSING LEARNING

As you observe the children in your classroom while they respond to books through talk and play, the notes and anecdotal records you collect will become valuable tools for understanding how your students are constructing and using their literacy knowledge in the responsive play context:

- *Responsive play checklists* can be analyzed for growth and development by looking for more check marks on more topics over time, demonstrating learning.
- *Responsive play anecdotal records* can be analyzed for themes. (For example, Tianna may consistently demonstrate the ways that she is familiar with various phonemic awareness and phonics concepts as she plays with others and helps them read, as she did with Dahlia, demonstrating knowledge and learning of these topics.)
- Detailed responsive play notes can be analyzed for themes in more detail. (For example, a student may retell stories in many responsive play engagements using various vocabulary words learned in class, demonstrating language/literacy development over time.)

- *Responsive playwatching forms* can be analyzed in all of these ways. Further, teachers can analyze their own thinking about students' reading motivations, use of strategies, and demonstrations of skills as they reread their own notes and critical reflections about the play engagements.

Documenting and analyzing various aspects of children's literacies as they play in response to books will allow you to move *beyond* standard literacy testing protocols (such as paper-and-pencil tests) and toward a more comprehensive approach that values children's histories, experiences, and knowledge. By engaging in responsive playwatching and systematically analyzing your observational documentation, you will be able to assess and understand what your students know about:

- Book handling
- Print awareness (concepts of letters and words, reading directionality)
- The functions/uses of written language
- Phonemic awareness and phonics (alphabet and word knowledge)
- Making personal and intertextual connections
- Retelling stories
- Extending stories
- Making predictions
- Story comprehension
- Sequence of events
- Story settings
- Characters
- The connections between readers, authors, and illustrators
- Language use and vocabulary
- Students' book preferences

Building on Children's Knowledge

Understanding what your students *know* will also help you understand what they might *need*. By observing who your students are, what they know, what they can do in your classroom, and what they enjoy, you can affirm the legitimacy of their knowledge and experiences and use these to craft meaningful classroom instruction that builds from and on their ways of knowing and being.

Consider the vignette highlighted in Chapter 3 wherein Bianca and Kaylee read and play with(in) the *Thunderstorm* book. In this example, we see that the students recall learning about clocks in the classroom and "become" the clocks in the story as they act out the scenes together. As a teacher, you can use this! You can share this responsive play example with the class and use the book as a prompt for continuing lessons on telling time, allowing children to become the clocks in the story—connecting math, reading, and play.

Similarly, think about the vignette (also in Chapter 3) wherein Alyssa and Maya read *Creepy Carrots* and then create an extended alternate ending to the story in which the rabbit character gets revenge on the carrots. This example can be shared and possibly (re)played with the class and can also act as a writing prompt (more about this is shared in Chapter 5). This would connect reading, writing, and playing in ways that can simultaneously motivate your students *and* support their learning.

Building on children's responsive play in these ways values students' knowledge as an important component of the classroom learning landscape. Drawing on their experiences and playful responses to stories in these ways can make learning fun and meaningful for your students. Using children's knowledge and experiences can also provide responsive play exemplars that you can share with parents and administrators to highlight the ways that play–literacy connections support children's learning and development in your classroom.

FINAL THOUGHTS

This chapter has highlighted details about the importance of observing your students as they play with(in) books. It has also shared information about various ways to effectively observe the children in your classroom, including:

- Kidwatching
- Playwatching
- Responsive playwatching

Further, this chapter has outlined information about why it is important that you carefully document your observations of children's responsive play. Documentation details and resources that can help you on your responsive play journey were also shared and include:

- Responsive play checklists
- Responsive play anecdotal record
- Detailed responsive play notes
- Responsive playwatching form

Your careful observations and corresponding documentation will support you as you aim to provide valuable evidence of your students' learning to parents and administrators.

Finally, this chapter shared how to use your observations and documentation to build on children's knowledge and experiences to create meaningful and playful learning opportunities in your classroom.

Self-Evaluation

Beyond observing, documenting, analyzing, and assessing students learning as they engage in responsive play in the ways noted above, you should also consider *self-evaluation*. Self-evaluation is important because it can help your students reflect critically and think about what they are learning. It is also important for *you* as you think about the ways in which you support and facilitate your students' learning and development.

Students

As you (re)play engagements with students in your classroom (as noted in Chapter 3) or simply have discussions with children about their responsive play, consider also sharing your responsive play observations and documentation with them. Sharing what *you* noticed about their learning and their reading, talk, and play can encourage your students to self-evaluate by recognizing and reflecting on what they are able to do.

You can support children to self-evaluate by guiding them to ask themselves the following:

- What do I know?
  - How am I sharing what I know through responsive play?
- What am I good at? (reading, speaking, listening, playing, supporting peers)
- What am I learning?
  - How am I showing this through my responsive play?
- What can I do differently/try next time?

You (as a Teacher)

Similarly, you can ask yourself critical questions as you reflect on your observations, analyses, and assessment of your students' responsive play. Questions for your own self-evaluation can include:

- What is working?
  - What is not working? How can I fix this?
- What books do children enjoy/use? Should I change what books are used?
  - What materials do children enjoy/use? Should I change what materials are used?
- Do the children have enough time/space to read and play together?
- Am I noticing and valuing the students' knowledge and experiences?
- How can I better support children to show and share what they know?
- Am I building on children's responsive play engagements to create meaningful learning experiences/lessons?
  - How can I do this/improve?

Young children are brilliant. They are able to recognize what they know, what they do well, and ways that they can improve. If you engage in and facilitate self-evaluation in your classroom, you will help students, parents, and administrators recognize how responsive play simultaneously demonstrates and supports classroom learning in various ways. In the final chapter, you will be encouraged to build on these critical reflections and evaluations in order to further support children's play–literacy connections in your classroom.

5

✢

Play(ing) across the Day

The previous chapters in this book have highlighted the importance of providing opportunities for young children to respond to stories through play. They have suggested that teachers like yourself may need to think about ways to (re)build your classroom library, construct classroom spaces that allow children to engage in responsive play in both joyful and academic ways, and document and analyze children's playful responses to books in order to inform your classroom instruction.

In this closing chapter, you are encouraged to further support classroom literacy learning by implementing playful writing practices that build on responsive play. This chapter also invites you to "play across the day" by incorporating play across content areas and making space for children's digital play in your classroom. The chapter concludes with some final thoughts on sparking imaginative learning at school.

PLAYFUL WRITING

While formalizing play practices in the classroom context *may* lead to the colonization of children's play for school purposes and to a loss of authenticity, creating opportunities for children to learn through play in your classroom in relevant and genuine ways can *support* academic learning and instruction (Larson & Peterson, 2013). In fact, as you have seen throughout this book, children's abilities to engage in play in the classroom can have *direct* impacts on their learning.

Beyond including responsive play in your literacy instruction to foster your students' reading development and joy, you can further support authentic play–literacy connections in your classroom by incorporating playful writing options. Research suggests that play is a major contributor to children's development of written language (Vygotsky, 1978). In the classroom context, it is important to give children meaningful opportunities to draw from their knowledge, histories, and experiences (including their playful reading engagements) to help them explore writing.

Building on Responsive Play

As seen in the vignettes throughout this book, children's responsive play helps them understand stories, create their own storylines, extend stories, analyze characters, use reading strategies, and consider story structure and elements. Responsive play thus offers a useful framework for the development of language and literacy. It is also a powerful site for children to develop as capable authors, bringing their expertise to stories through their play.

The responsive play framework provides children with a meaningful context for taking risks and trying out new ideas in their playful responses to stories. As they play out various aspects of the books they read together, children become active participants of the stories on the pages. They also become story makers, motivated to write letters, words, and sentences and to compose and share their stories with others. In this sense, responsive play helps children explore stories in ways that provide a foundation for moving into putting *their* words on paper and becoming the authors of their *own* stories (Owocki, 1999).

For example, in Chapter 3, when Alyssa and Maya read *Creepy Carrots* together and respond playfully by extending the story ending, they become collaborative authors of their own imaginative story. Their creative reinterpretation of the *Creepy Carrots* book allows them to imagine and draft a playful otherwise (Flint & Adams, 2024). To incorporate writing and build on the responsive play story extension created by Alyssa and Maya, you could provide them with materials to write out and illustrate this new ending.

Their version of the story could then be shared with the class (they could read it, or you could read it to the class). As mentioned in Chapters 3 and 4, the story could then be (re)played, once with the original ending and then again with the new story ending written by Alyssa and Maya. These could then be discussed (compared/contrasted, analyzed, questioned) as a class, deepening literacy engagement and learning.

Similarly, when Logan, Diego, and Daniella respond to the *Thunderstorm* book, Logan narrates the story as if it is the tale *Three Little Pigs*, connecting and intertwining the two stories in imaginative and creative ways. After observing this responsive play session, you could provide the group with writing materials to draft the new story they played out. This could also be shared with/read to the class and (re)played, as noted above.

Children's playful responses to stories and their story (re)interpretations and extensions can prompt their writing, simultaneously connecting reading, writing, and responsive play in the classroom in meaningful ways. You can collect these stories and store them in a folder/binder, place them in your responsive play space, and allow children to read and respond to them through play, just as they would with any other story or book.

Essentially, providing students with opportunities for meaningful writing and (re)playing during and/or after responsive play sessions can support students' writing motivation, engagement, and development. Similar to responsive play, it is important that you:

- Make time for writing
- Create space(s) for writing
- Invite students to connect reading, responsive play, and writing
- Provide various writing materials that are easy to access; consider adding writing materials to your responsive play space
- Provide opportunities for students to share their writing
- Provide opportunities for students to listen to and read each other's writing
- Provide opportunities for students to respond to each other's writing through discussion, playing, and (re)playing
- Make time to observe responsive play to support students' writing
- Draw from and build on your responsive play observations to support and inform your writing instruction/lessons

Interweaving reading, responsive play, and writing in these ways can support children's joyful literacy learning and development.

PLAYING INTO THE FUTURE

As highlighted throughout the previous chapters, play is an essential component of childhood *and* of classroom learning. Beyond implementing responsive play and playful writing in your literacy instruction, joy, fun, engagement, and playfulness can be infused into and across your school day in various ways.

Play across Content Areas

You might be wondering how you can move beyond implementing responsive play and playful writing into making play the *center* of the curriculum across content areas. You have likely used play in your classroom to support content area objectives in various ways before, but what if you focus on the ways that curricula can support and enrich your students' play instead? When we flip the perspective in this way, we place play at the center of learning.

A play-centered curriculum can provide rich context for the development of children's mathematical, scientific, and artistic thinking. Young children often spontaneously deepen their understandings of various concepts through their playful hands-on investigations and engagements. Children also think across content areas as they use their developing abilities and knowledge to think about and solve real-world problems through play (Van Hoorn et al., 2015).

Providing opportunities for your students to play spontaneously and to engage in play that is guided by you (focused on content area topics) allows children to use their emerging abilities and problem-solving skills in meaningful contexts. A play-centered curriculum can build on your students' lives, experiences, and interests and can help deepen their understandings as they use their emerging skills to solve problems they confront during their playful explorations and engagements.

Here are some ways to center play in your curriculum across content areas (math, science, art, social studies):

- Provide various opportunities for children to play together during content area instruction and throughout the day (responsive play, spontaneous play, and teacher-guided play)
- Observe children's play throughout the day to connect learning opportunities:
  - Connect content area instruction to children's lives and routines, including (and especially) their play
  - Connect play topics noticed during play observations to content area instruction
  - Connect topics across content areas (connect math-literacy, science-math, art-social studies) through play and exploration, guided by students' interests
- Provide hands-on tools and manipulatives for children to play with and explore during content area instruction and throughout the day. For example, children can do the following:
  - Create objects/items with Play-Doh or clay
  - Play with, explore, build, and create with blocks and Legos

- Play with and explore various items/materials (water, sand, blocks, buttons, beans, books, photographs)
- Play with, observe, and examine objects/items and their features (with magnifying glasses, rulers)
- Explore and play with nature (plants, leaves, sand, water, gravity, air)
- Paint
- Draw
- Write
- Discuss various topics
- Make and tinker with objects/artifacts (in makerspaces)
- Play with and explore technology and digital tools

Digital Play

Beyond incorporating playful opportunities across content areas and providing various materials to center play across your classroom instruction, it is also important to support children's digital literacies and play in your classroom (as highlighted in the final bullet point above).

Children's digital literacies include reading, writing, and multimodal literacy practices that incorporate important and meaningful technologies, media, and popular culture texts/artifacts and are often demonstrated through children's digital play (Flint & Adams, 2024; Wood et al., 2019).

With(in) and through their digital play, young children often use imaginary items to make sense of their worlds in which digital technologies are important artifacts (Bird, 2019). Correspondingly, there is a connected and reciprocal relationship between children and the real and imagined digital objects and materials that they play with (Burnett et al., 2014; Lundtofte et al., 2019). It is through these connections and relationships—demonstrated through their digital play—where children's digital (and other) identities can develop and "become."

This highlights the *fluidity* of children's identities, suggesting that they can shift over time and with(in) and across spaces in important ways (Kuby & Vaughn, 2015; Yoon, 2014). These findings connect to sociocultural frameworks, as noted in this book's Introduction, which similarly suggest that social practices and artifacts, including real/imagined digital devices and content, create a shared system for children's participation, meaning making, and identity construction (Kumpulainen & Renshaw, 2007).

Connecting Responsive and Digital Play

Children are surrounded by technology. They live, learn, and grow in increasingly digital contexts and environments. Digital play, in the classroom setting, gives children opportunities to *play around* with digital tools and identities in meaningful ways. It is important that you provide space and opportunities for digital play in your classroom and that you build on young children's joyful ways of knowing, being, and becoming within their digital world(s).

To connect responsive play and digital play in your classroom, consider:

- Adding digital texts to your responsive play library
- Providing digital objects, toys, and materials for children to use/play with during responsive play
- Providing digital tools, cameras, iPads, and recording devices for children to record and document responsive play sessions in various ways
- Facilitating digital editing of recorded sessions
- (Re)watching, listening to, discussing, and (re)playing recorded sessions with children to facilitate critical discussions and inquiries
- Observing and documenting children's digital responsive play
- Collecting and storing responsive play photographs, recordings, and documentation to share with children to facilitate critical discussions and to use as writing prompts
- Encouraging and facilitating critical conversations with students about media and popular culture (body image, ideals of beauty, character portrayals, gender, race, roles) related to books/stories and responsive play engagements
- Drawing from and building on children's digital responsive play to support and inform your classroom instruction

Encourage and support your students as they play with and explore technology and as they expertly narrate and (re)invent stories through their digital play in creative and imaginative ways (Wohlwend, 2013a).

FINAL, FINAL THOUGHTS

This chapter has briefly outlined how you can center play in the curriculum and how you can further support your students' playful learning by:

- Building on responsive play to incorporating playful writing
- Playing across content areas and across the school day
- Connecting children's digital and responsive play

These are just a few ways that you can incorporate and center play throughout the school day and build on responsive play to support and inform your literacy instruction. This book will now close with some final, final thoughts on the importance of drawing from children's sense of curiosity and wonder in the classroom.

Sparking Imaginative Learning

John Dewey, one of the most influential minds of the twentieth century, laments the "open-minded and flexible wonder of childhood and the ease with which this endowment is lost" (Dewey, 1910, p. 33). He suggests that, with respect to children's sense of curiosity, the teacher's task is to "keep alive the sacred spark of wonder and to fan the flame that already glows" (Dewey, 1910, p. 34). Education, according to Dewey, should (re)kindle imaginative learning and draw from and build on children's sense of curiosity and wonder.

Remember Tom Hanks's character from the movie *Castaway* that was discussed in the introduction of this book, joyously fanning the flames of the fire that would sustain him on the deserted island? Just like this character who spent hours tending to a small spark until it caught fire, teachers must, as Dewey suggests, keep the spark of children's wonder alive and fan the flames of curiosity that always, already burns within them.

Children's play in response to stories is curious, joyful, and wondrous—a spark. This book suggests several ways that you can tend to that joyful spark and fan it into a raging fire of imaginative literacy learning in your classroom. As noted throughout these chapters, it is important to remember that, for instruction to be effective and impactful, the students in your classroom must "have opportunities to play, to be wildly imaginative, and to laugh" (Garcia & Morrell, 2022, p. 58).

It is my hope that you can (re)kindle playful and joyful learning in your classroom and that you "keep alive" your students' sacred spark of wonder by supporting them as they read and respond to books and stories together in wildly imaginative and playful ways.

References

Adomat, D. S. (2009). Actively engaging with stories through drama: Portraits of two young readers. *The Reading Teacher, 62*, 628–636.

ALTEC at the University of Kansas. (2008). Classroom Architect [Computer software]. http://classroom.4teachers.org

Bakhtin, M. M. (1986). *Speech genres and other late essays* (V. W. McGee, Trans.). University of Texas Press.

Bird, J. (2019). "You need a phone and camera in your bag before you go out!": Children's play with imaginative technologies. *British Journal of Educational Technology, 51*(1), 166–176.

Bishop, R. S. (1990). Mirrors, windows, and sliding glass doors. *Perspectives: Choosing and Using Books for the Classroom, 6*(3), ix–xi.

Bishop, R. S. (2016). A ride with Nana and CJ: Engagement, appreciation, and social action. *Language Arts, 94*(2), 120.

Blaise, M. (2005). *Playing it straight: Uncovering gender discourses in the early childhood classroom*. Routledge.

Bodrova, E., & Leong, D. J. (2007). *Tools of the mind: The Vygotskian approach to early childhood education*. Pearson.

Boldt, G., & Leander, K. M. (2020). Affect theory in reading research: Imagining the radical difference. *Reading Psychology, 41*(6), 515–532.

Boushey, G., & Moser, J. (2006). *The daily five*. Stenhouse.

Burnett, C., Merchant, G., Pahl, K., & Rowsell, J. (2014). The (im)materiality of literacy: The significance of subjectivity to new literacies research. *Discourse: Studies in the Cultural Politics of Education, 35*(1), 90–103.

Christie, J. F., & Roskos, K. A. (2009). Play's potential in early literacy development. *Encyclopedia on Early Childhood Development*, 1–6. http://www.childencyclopedia.com/documents/Christie-RoskosANGxp.pdf

References

Davies, B., & Banks, C. (1992). The gender trap: A feminist poststructuralist analysis of primary school children's talk about gender. *Journal of Curriculum Studies, 24*(1), 1–25.

Dernikos, B. P. (2020). Tuning into rebellious matter: Affective literacies as more-than-human sonic bodies. *English Teaching: Practice and Critique, 19*(4), 417–432.

Dewey, J. (1910). *How we think*. D. C. Heath.

Dewey, J. (1938). *Experience and education*. Simon & Schuster.

Dreyfus, H. L., & Wrathall, M. A. (Eds.). (2007). *A companion to Heidegger* (Vol. 50). John Wiley & Sons.

Dutro, E. (2003). "Us boys like to read football and boy stuff": Reading masculinities, performing boyhood. *Journal of Literacy Research, 34*(4), 465–500.

Dyson, A. H. (1994). The Ninjas, the X-Men, and the Ladies: Playing with power and identity in an urban primary school. *Teachers College Record, 96*, 219–239.

Dyson, A. H. (1996). Cultural constellations and childhood identities: On Greek gods, cartoon heroes, and the social lives of schoolchildren. *Harvard Educational Review, 66*, 471–495.

Edmiston (Enciso), P. (1990). *The nature of engagement in reading: Profiles of three fifth graders' engagement strategies and stances*. Unpublished doctoral dissertation, Ohio State University.

Enciso, P. (1996). Why engagement in reading matters to Molly. *Reading & Writing Quarterly: Overcoming Learning Difficulties, 12*(2), 171–194.

Enciso, P. (2021). "Where are you?": Reading, repositioning, and imagining for antiracist future. In D. Sumara & D. E. Alvermann (Eds.), *Ideas that changed literacy practices: First person accounts from leading voices* (pp. 93–102). Myers Education Press.

Flint, T. K. (2016). *Responsive play: Exploring play as reader response in a first grade classroom* (Doctoral dissertation, University of Arizona). ProQuest Dissertations and Theses Global.

Flint, T. K. (2020a). Children's critical reflections on gender and beauty through responsive play in the classroom context. *Early Childhood Education Journal, 48*(6), 739–749.

Flint, T. K. (2020b). Responsive play: Creating transformative classroom spaces through play as reader response. *Journal of Early Childhood Literacy, 20*(2), 385–410.

Flint, T. K., & Adams, M. (2018). "It's like playing, but learning": Supporting early literacy development through responsive play with wordless picturebooks. *Language Arts, 96*(1), 21–36.

Flint, T. K., & Adams, M. S. (2024). Of ladles and laptops: Exploring preschool children's digital play. *Early Childhood Education Journal, 52*, 1001–1010.

Galda, L., & Liang, L. A. (2003). Literature as experience or looking for facts: Stance in the classroom. *Reading Research Quarterly, 38*(2), 268–275.

Garcia, A., & Morrell, E. (2022). *Tuned-in teaching: Centering youth culture for an active and just classroom*. Heinemann.

Gaskins, S. (2014). Children's play as cultural activity. In L. Brooker, M. Glaise, & S. Edwards (Eds.), *The Sage handbook of play and learning in early childhood* (pp. 31–42). Sage.

Gee, J. P. (2012). *Social linguistics and literacies: Ideology in discourses* (4th ed.). Routledge.

Gonzalez, N., Moll, L. C., & Amanti, C. (2005). *Funds of knowledge: Theorizing practices in households, communities, and classrooms*. Routledge.

Heath, S. B. (1983). *Ways with words: Language, life, and work in communities and classrooms*. Cambridge University Press.

Jiménez, L. M. (2021). Mirrors and windows with texts and readers: Intersectional social justice at work in the classroom. *Language Arts, 98*(3), 156–161.

Keefer, N., & Flint, T. K. (2023). Women's rights issues and literacy: Theory, research, and practice. In N. Keefer & J. Clabough (Eds.), *Thematic teaching of women's rights issues with social studies trade books* (pp. 15–30). Lexington Books.

Kress, G. (2003). *Literacy in the new media age*. Routledge.

Kuby, C. R., & Vaughn, M. (2015). Young children's identities becoming: Exploring agency in the creation of multimodal literacies. *Journal of Early Childhood Literacy, 15*(4), 433–472.

Kumpulainen, K., & Renshaw, P. (2007). Cultures of learning. *International Journal of Educational Research, 46*(3–4), 109–115.

Kumpulainen, K., Sairanen, H., & Nordström, A. (2020). Young children's digital literacy practices in the sociocultural contexts of their homes. *Journal of Early Childhood Literacy, 20*(3), 472–499.

Larson, J., & Peterson, S. (2013). Talk and discourse in formal learning settings. In J. Larson & J. Marsh (Eds.), *The Sage handbook of early childhood literacy* (pp. 501–539). Sage.

Lave, J., & Wenger, E. (1991). *Situated learning: Legitimate peripheral participation*. Cambridge University Press.

Leander, K. M., & Boldt, G. (2013). Rereading "A pedagogy of multiliteracies": Bodies, texts, and emergence. *Journal of Literacy Research, 45*(1), 22–46.

Leander, K. M., & Rowe, D. W. (2006). Mapping literacy spaces in motion: A rhizomatic analysis of a classroom literacy performance. *Reading Research Quarterly, 41*, 428–460.

Lundtofte, T. E., Odgaard, A. B., & Skovbjerg, H. M. (2019). Absorbency and utensilency: A spectrum for analysing children's digital play practices. *Global Studies of Childhood, 9*(4), 335–347.

Marsh, J. (2017). The Internet of toys: A posthuman and multimodal analysis of connected play. *Teachers College Record, 119*(12), 1–32.

Marsh, J. (2000). 'But I want to fly too!': Girls and superhero play in the infant classroom. *Gender and Education, 12*(2), 209–220.

Marshall, E. (2016). Counter-storytelling through graphic life writing. *Language Arts, 94*(2), 79–93.

Moll, L. C. (1992). Bilingual classroom studies and community analysis: Some recent trends. *Educational Researcher, 21*(2), 20–24.

Muhammad, G. (2023). *Unearthing joy: A guide to culturally and historically responsive teaching and learning*. Scholastic.

Myers, C. (2014, March 15). The apartheid of children's literature. *New York Times*. https://www.nytimes.com/2014/03/16/opinion/sunday/the-apartheid-of-childrensliterature.html

New London Group. (1996). A pedagogy of multiliteracies: Designing social futures. *Harvard Electronic Review, 66*(1), 60–93.

Nourot, P. M. (1998). Sociodramatic play: Pretending together. In D. P. Fromberg & D. Bergen (Eds.), *Play from birth to twelve and beyond: Contexts, perspectives, and meanings* (pp. 165–174). Garland Publishing.

O'Keefe, T. (1997). The habit of kidwatching. *School Talk, 3*(2), 4–6.

Owocki, G. (1999). *Literacy through play*. Heinemann.

Owocki, G., & Goodman, Y. (2002). *Kidwatching: Documenting children's literacy development*. Heinemann.

Pahl, K., & Rowsell, J. (2010). *Artifactual literacies: Every object tells a story*. Teachers College Press.

Paley, V. G. (1984). *Boys and girls: Superheroes in the doll corner*. University of Chicago Press.

Paley, V. G. (2004). *A child's work: The importance of fantasy play*. University of Chicago Press.

Pantaleo, S. (2008). *Exploring student response to contemporary picturebooks*. University of Toronto Press.

Riojas-Cortez, M. (2001). Preschoolers' funds of knowledge displayed through sociodramatic play episodes in a bilingual classroom. *Early Childhood Education Journal, 29*(1), 35–40.

Rosenblatt, L. M. (1938). *Literature as exploration*. Modern Language Association of America.

Rosenblatt, L. M. (1978). *The reader, the text, the poem: The transactional theory of the literary work*. Southern Illinois University Press.

Rowe, A. (1996). Voices off: Reading wordless picture books. In M. Styles, E. Bearne, & V. Watson (Eds.), *Voices off: Texts, contexts, and readers* (pp. 219–234). Continuum International Publishing Group.

Rowe, D. W. (1998). The literate potentials of book-related dramatic play. *Reading Research Quarterly, 33*(1), 10–35.

Rowe, D. W. (2007). Bringing books to life: The role of book-related dramatic play in young children's literacy learning. In K. Roskos & J. Christie (Eds.), *Play and literacy in early childhood: Research from multiple perspectives* (2nd ed., pp. 37–63). Lawrence Erlbaum Associates.

Ryan, C. L., & Hermann-Wilmarth, J. M. (2018). *Reading the rainbow: LGBTQ-inclusive literacy instruction in the elementary classroom*. Teachers College Press.

Saracho, O. N., & Spodek, B. (2006). Young children's literacy-related play. *Early Child Development and Care, 176*(7), 707–721.

Sawyer, R. K., & DeZutter, S. (2017). Improvisation: A lens for play and literacy research. In K. Roskos & J. Christie (Eds.), *Play and literacy in early childhood: Research from multiple perspectives* (2nd ed., pp. 21–36). Lawrence Erlbaum Associates.

Sipe, L. R. (2008). *Storytime: Young children's literary understanding in the classroom*. Teachers College Press.

Thiel, J. J. (2015). "Bumblebee's in trouble!" Embodied literacies during imaginative superhero play. *Language Arts, 93*(1), 38–49.

Toliver, S. R. (2021). On mirrors, windows, and telescopes. *Council Chronicle, 31*(1), 29–30.

Van Hoorn, J., Nourot, P. M., Scales, B., & Alward, K. R. (2015). *Play at the center of the curriculum* (6th ed.). Pearson.

Vygotsky, L. S. (1978). *Mind in society: The development of higher psychological processes*. Harvard University Press.

Wells, G. (1986). *The meaning makers: Children learning language and using language to learn*. Heinemann.

Wood, E., Nuttall, J., Edwards, S., & Grieshaber, S. (2019). Young children's digital play in early childhood settings: Curriculum, pedagogy and teachers' knowledge. In *The Routledge handbook of digital literacies in early childhood* (pp. 214–226). Routledge.

Wohlwend, K. E. (2011). *Playing their way into literacies: Reading, writing, and belonging in the early childhood classroom*. Teachers College Press.

Wohlwend, K. E. (2012). "Are you guys girls?": Boys, identity texts, and Disney princess play. *Journal of Early Childhood Literacy, 12*(1), 3–23.

Wohlwend, K. E. (2013a). *Literacy playshop: New literacies, popular media, and play in the early childhood classroom*. Teachers College Press.

Wohlwend, K. E. (2013b). Play, literacies, and the converging cultures of childhood. In J. Larson & J. Marsh (Eds.), *The Sage handbook of early childhood literacy* (pp. 80–110). Sage.

Wohlwend, K. E. (2023). Serious play for serious times: Recentering play in early literacy classrooms. *The Reading Teacher, 76*(4), 478–486.

Yoon, H. S. (2014). Can I play with you? The intersection of play and writing in a kindergarten classroom. *Contemporary Issues in Early Childhood, 15*(2), 109–121.

CHILDREN'S LITERATURE REFERENCES

Argueta, J. (2007). *A movie in my pillow: Una pelicula en mi almohada* (E. Gomez, Illus.). Children's Book Press.

Bailey, J. (2019). *A friend for Henry* (M. Song, Illus.). Chronicle Books.

Baker, J. (2010). *Mirror*. Candlewick.

Barnes, D. (2017). *Crown: An ode to the fresh cut* (G. C. James, Illus.). Bolden, Agate Publishing.

Barnes, D. (2020). *I am every good thing* (G. C. James, Illus.). Nancy Paulsen Books.

Bauer, M. D. (2018). *The stuff of stars* (E. Holmes, Illus.). Candlewick.

Beaty, D. (2013). *Knock, knock: My dad's dream for me* (B. Collier, Illus.). Little, Brown Books for Young Readers.

Becker, A. (2013). *Journey*. Candlewick.

Blackburne, L. (2021). *I dream of Popo*. Roaring Brook Press.

Boyd, L. (2014). *Flashlight*. Chronicle Books.

Brown, M. (2011). *Marisol McDonald doesn't match/Marisol McDonald no combina* (S. Palacios, Illus.). Children's Book Press.

Bryant, J. (2013). *A splash of red: The life and art of Horace Pippin* (M. Sweet, Illus.). Knopf Books for Young Readers.

Byers, G. (2018). *I am enough* (K. A. Bobo, Illus.). Balzer + Bray.

Cherry, M. A. (2019). *Hair love* (V. Harrison, Illus.). Kokila.

Choi, Y. (2003). *The name jar*. Dragonfly Books.
Cole, H. (2022). *Forever home: A dog and boy love story*. Scholastic Press.
Colón, R. (2014). *Draw!* Simon & Schuster/Paula Wiseman Books.
Cordell, M. (2017). *Wolf in the snow*. Feiwel & Friends.
Davidson, S. F., & Davidson, R. (2022). *Dancing with our ancestors* (J. Gibbons, Illus.). HighWater Press.
Deedy, C. A. (2014). *Martina the beautiful cockroach: A Cuban folktale* (M. Austin, Illus.). Peachtree.
De la Peña, M. (2015). *Last stop on Market Street* (C. Robinson, Illus.). G. P. Putnam's Sons Books for Young Readers.
Del Rizzo, S. (2021). *Birds on Wishbone Street*. Pajama Press.
dePaola, T. (2018). *Pancakes for breakfast*. Clarion Books.
Diaz, J. (2018). *Islandborn* (L. Espinosa, Illus.). Dial Books.
Diaz, L. (2021). *Paletero man* (M. Player, Illus.). HarperCollins.
Dorros, A. (1997). *Abuela* (E. Klevin, Illus.). Puffin Books.
Erdrich, L. (2020). *The range eternal* (S. Johnson & L. Fancher, Illus.). University of Minnesota Press.
Ehrenberg, P. (2017). *Queen of the Hanukkah dosas* (A. Sarkar, Illus.). Farrar, Straus and Giroux.
Flett, J. (2019). *Birdsong*. Greystone Kids.
Ford, J. R., & Ford, V. (2021). *Calvin* (K. Harren, Illus.). G. P. Putnam's Sons Books for Young Readers.
Gale, H. (2019). *Ho'onani: Hula warrior* (M. Song, Illus.). Tundra Books.
Garza, C. L. (2017). *Lucia the luchadora* (A. Bermudez, Illus.). POW! Kids Books.
Geisert, A. (2013). *Thunderstorm*. Enchanted Lion Books.
Gonzales, M. (2017). *Yo soy Muslim: A father's letter to his daughter* (M. Amini, Illus.). Salaam Reads.
González, K. N. (2022). *The coquíes still sing: A story of home, hope, and rebuilding* (K. Quiles, Illus.). Roaring Brook Press.
González, X. (2022). *Where wonder grows* (A. M. Garcia, Illus.). Cinco Puntos Press.
Goodluck, L. (2024). *Too much: My great big Native family* (B. George, Illus.). Simon & Schuster Books for Young Readers.
Griffin, D. (2020). *Shine* (L. Bobbiesi, Illus.). Tyndale House Publishers.
Ho, J. (2021). *Eyes that kiss in the corners* (D. Ho, Illus.). HarperCollins.
Hoffman, M. (1991). *Amazing Grace* (C. Binch, Illus.). Dial Books.
Hourigan, E. (2022). *In the blue*. Little, Brown Books for Young Readers.
Idle, M. (2013). *Flora and the flamingo*. Chronicle Books.
Iglesias, J. P. (2019). *Daniel and Ismail* (A. Peris, Illus.). Yonder.
Janicki, P. (2023). *The secret pocket* (C. Victor, Illus.). Orca Book Publishers.
Keats, E. J. (1962). *The snowy day*. Viking Books for Young Readers.
Lê, M. (2018). *Drawn together* (D. Santat, Illus.). Little, Brown Books for Young Readers.
Lê, M. (2022). *The Blur* (D. Santat, Illus.). Knopf Books for Young Readers.
Lebeuf, D. (2021). *My city speaks* (A. Barron, Illus.). Kids Can Press.
Lee, J. (2015). *Pool*. Chronicle Books.
Lee, S. (2008). *Wave*. Chronicle Books.
Lehman, B. (2004). *The red book*. Clarion Books.

Lester, H. (2002). *Hooway for Wodney Wat* (L. Munsinger, Illus.). Clarion Books.
Leung, J. (2023). *The truth about dragons* (H. Cha, Illus.). Henry Holt and Co.
Lin, G. (2014). *Dim sum for everyone!* Knopf Books for Young Readers.
Lindstrom, C. (2020). *We are water protectors* (M. Goade, Illus.). Roaring Brook Press.
Lindstrom, C. (2023). *My powerful hair* (S. Littlebird, Illus.). Harry N. Abrams.
Lyon, G. E. (2010). *The pirate of kindergarten* (L. Avril, Illus.). Atheneum/Richard Jackson Books.
Maillard, K. N. (2019). *Fry bread* (J. Martinez, Illus.). Roaring Brook Press.
Masurel, C. (2000). *Ten dogs in the window: A countdown book* (P. Paparone, Illus.). North-South Books (Houghton Mifflin Big Book Series).
McGinty, A. B. (2022). *Bathe the cat* (D. Roberts, Illus.). Chronicle Books.
Mercurio, P. (2020). *Our subway baby* (L. Espinosa, Illus.). Dial Books.
Mishra-Newbery, U., & Al-Hathloul, L. (2022). *Loujain dreams of sunflowers* (R. Green, Illus.). minedition.
Miyares, D. (2015). *Float*. Simon & Schuster Books for Young Readers.
Morales, A. (2021). *Areli is a dreamer* (L. Uribe, Illus.). Random House Studio.
Morales, Y. (2018). *Dreamers*. Neal Porter Books.
Morales, Y. (2015). *Niño wrestles the world*. Square Fish.
Muhammad, I. (2019). *The proudest blue* (S. K. Ali Hatem Aly, Illus.). Little, Brown Books for Young Readers.
Munsch, R. N. (1980). *The paper bag princess* (M. Martchenko, Illus.). Annick Press.
Neal, T., & Neal, D. (2020). *My rainbow* (A. Twink, Illus.). Kokila.
Nyong'o, L. (2019). *Sulwe* (V. Harrison, Illus.). Simon & Schuster Books for Young Readers.
Oliveros, J. (2018). *The remember balloons* (D. Wulfekotte, Illus.). Simon & Schuster Books for Young Readers.
Phi, B., & Tran, N. D. B. (2019). *My footprints*. Capstone Editions.
Pinkney, J. (2009). *The lion and the mouse*. Little, Brown Books for Young Readers.
Pinkwater, D. (2010). *Beautiful Yetta: The Yiddish chicken* (J. Pinkwater, Illus.). Feiwel & Friends.
Pitman, G. E. (2018). *Sewing the rainbow: A story about Gilbert Baker* (H. Clifton Brown, Illus.). Magination Press.
Polacco, P. (1994). *Mrs. Katz and Tush*. Dragonfly Books.
Polacco, P. (2009). *The butterfly*. Philomel Books.
Quintero, I. (2019). *My papi has a motorcycle* (Z. Peña, Illus.). Kokila.
Rahman, B. (2021). *A sky-blue bench* (P. Collins, Illus.). Pajama Press.
Recorvits, H. (2014). *My name is Yoon* (G. Swiatkowska, Illus.). Square Fish.
Reibstein, M. (2008). *Wabi Sabi* (E. Young, Illus.). Little, Brown Books for Young Readers.
Reynolds, A., & Brown, P. (2012). *Creepy carrots*. Simon & Schuster.
Richardson, J., & Parnell, P. (2005). *And Tango makes three*. Simon & Schuster Books for Young Readers.
Ringgold, F. (1996). *Tar beach*. Dragonfly Books.
Robertson, D. (2021). *On the trapline* (J. Fett, Illus.). Tundra Books.
Robinson, C. (2019). *Another*. Atheneum Books for Young Readers.

Rogers, A. L. (2024). *When we gather (Ostadahlisiha): A Cherokee tribal feast* (M. Goodnight, Illus.). Heartdrum.
Rohmann, E. (2002). *My friend Rabbit*. Roaring Brook Press.
Ruurs, M. M. (2016). *Stepping stones: A refugee family's journey* (F. Raheem, Trans.; N. A. Vadr, Illus.). Orca Book Publishers.
Salati, D. (2022). *Hot dog*. Knopf Books for Young Readers.
Say, A. (2008). *Grandfather's journey*. Clarion Books.
Scott, J. (2020). *I talk like a river* (S. Smith, Illus.). Neal Porter Books.
Shannon, D. (1998). *No, David!* The Blue Sky Press.
Sheth, K. (2013). *Tiger in my soup* (J. Ebbeler, Illus.). Peachtree Publishers.
Shihab Nye, N. (1997). *Sitti's secrets* (N. Carpenter, Illus.). Aladdin.
Smith, S. (2019). *Small in the city*. Neal Porter Books.
Soto, G. (1997). *Chato's kitchen* (S. Guevara, Illus.). Puffin Books.
Soto, G. (1996). *Too many tamales* (E. Martinez, Illus.). Puffin Books.
Stiefel, C. (2022). *The tower of life: How Yaffa Eliach rebuilt her town* (S. Gal, Illus.). Scholastic Press.
Stocker, S. (2022). *Listen: How Evelyn Glennie, a deaf girl, changed percussion* (D. Holzwarth, Illus.). Dial Books.
Talbott, H. (2021). *A walk in the words*. Nancy Paulsen Books.
Tan, S. (2007). *The arrival*. Arthur A. Levine Books.
Teague, M. (2019). *Fly*. Beach Lane Books.
Thompkins-Bigelow, J. (2022). *Abdul's story* (T. Rose, Illus.). Salaam Reads.
Thompson, B. (2010). *Chalk*. Two Lions.
Tregonning, M. (2021). *Small things*. Pajama Press.
Van den Ende, P. (2020). *The wanderer*. Levine Querido.
Wang, A. (2021). *Watercress* (J. Chin, Illus.). Neal Porter Books.
Wiesner, D. (1991). *Tuesday*. Clarion Books.
Wild, C. S. (2022). *Love, Violet* (C. Chua, Illus.). Farrar, Straus and Giroux.
Wing, N. (1996). *Jalepeño bagels* (R. Casilla, Illus.). Atheneum Books for Young Readers.
Woodgate, H. (2021). *Grandad's camper*. Little Bee Books.
Woodson, J. (2022). *The year we learned to fly* (R. López, Illus.). Nancy Paulsen Books.
Woodson, J. (2015). *Visiting day* (J. E. Ransome, Illus.). Nancy Paulsen Books.
Yan, K. K. (2021). *From the tops of the trees* (R. Wada, Illus.). Carolrhoda Books.

About the Author

Tori K. Flint began her career in Arizona, where she was a preschool teacher and then a first-grade teacher for many years. She went on to earn her PhD in language, reading, and culture with a focus on early literacy from the University of Arizona. Currently, she is an associate professor of literacy and early childhood education at the University of Louisiana at Lafayette. She is also the cofounder and codirector of the Louisiana Center for Research and Education on Languages and Literacies. Broadly, her research bridges early literacies, play, children's literature, and multimodality. She believes that education should be joyful and that we should listen to and learn from the brilliance of children.

www.ingramcontent.com/pod-product-compliance
Lightning Source LLC
Chambersburg PA
CBHW021813220426
43662CB00006B/292